CIDER BEANS, WILD GREENS, AND DANDELION JELLY

CIDER BEANS,
WILD GREENS, AND
DANDELION JELLY

Recipes from
Southern Appalachia

JOAN E. ALLER

Andrews McMeel
Publishing, LLC
Kansas City • Sydney • London

FOR **ELIZABETH OLSEN ALLER**
AND **FLORENCE BISCEGLIA OLSEN**,
TWO OF THE BEST COOKS I KNOW,

and for

BEVERLY HEINZLER,
WHO BELIEVES THAT WOMEN CAN

10 11 12 13 14 WKT 10 9 8 7 6 5 4 3 2 1

ISBN-13: 978-0-7407-7958-9
ISBN-10: 0-7407-7958-3

Library of Congress Control Number: 2009940830

Design by Vertigo Design NYC
Food photography by Ben Fink
Photo on page vi courtesy of The Hawkesdene House
Photo on page 132 courtesy of The Creekwalk Inn
Photos on pages 3, 5, 6, 8, 9, 40, 45, 108, and 170 courtesy of Joan E. Aller

www.andrewsmcmeel.com

Contents

Acknowledgments

⬦

I'M NOT SURE if anyone sits down one day and says, "I think I'll write a cookbook." Of course, I could be wrong. In the beginning, this book was about my local area, a view from my mountain "holler." It's been fortunate that I've had numerous people telling me stories, sharing recipes, and cheering me on, and as a result, what started out as a little book has grown to include all of southern Appalachia. Upon hearing of the book, folks talked to me as if I were their southern kin: "Ya'll have to go here" or "Ya'll have to talk to . . . ." The joy with which they share their heritage and their friendly spirit is part of what makes this region so special.

Lane Butler: No one writes a book alone, and it's the editor's job to make it all come together. That, Lane did beautifully. Her real talent lies in being able to communicate with an author and gently guide him or her along a set path. I'm not sure she'll ever know just how much I appreciate her and her guidance. My vision became her vision, and somewhere in the process of creating this book, it blossomed into something much grander than I had originally conceived. For that, and for so much more, I thank and acknowledge her.

Barbara Ward Land: One of my neighbors as the crow flies and a native southern Appalachian,

Barb is a trained pastry chef and an accomplished cook. A busy woman, she not only contributed to the book, but also put up with my popping up at any given moment, usually where she was working, asking her questions about certain recipes. She never failed to graciously help me.

Larry Ward: Larry is a fifth-generation woodworker and carver here in the southern Appalachian Mountains. His family has been featured in major works on the area, and Larry can tell you anything you'd want to know about the southern Appalachian culture. He once told me that "outsiders aren't going to find us by hanging out in town. They need to get out and talk to local folks." Larry is an outrageous storyteller and is responsible for the recipe for homemade Appalachian wines.

Robert Grannis: My friend Bob has been supportive and encouraging from the beginning. While I was sitting in the winter cold, he never failed to tell me the temperature in Florida. Ha! We share the belief that all cultures are valuable and should be honored, and I've attempted to do that in this book. No place is made up of just one kind of people, and we often overlook the contributions made and the shared histories. The gathering of different cultures gives southern Appalachia its unique flavor.

Errol Dillon: Errol, my Mississippi friend, encouraged my photography.

John C. Rivers: My southern Appalachian friend from Alabama, J.C. has contributed to the book by giving me his recipes and sharing his expertise on soul food. His family has been in the area since slavery and his knowledge of history and local sites is invaluable. His encouragement and contributions to the book have been gratefully received.

Bed-and-breakfast inns: I would also like to acknowledge the bed-and-breakfast inn owners and chefs who contributed to the book. Although I haven't yet met many of them in person, I found them to be warm and positive folks who did not hesitate to participate when asked. Some of them are native southern Appalachians and others have chosen the region as their home. They shared family recipes and stories along with their insights into the area.

Introduction

THE APPALACHIAN MOUNTAIN RANGES were the first to be formed on the American continent, and after eons, they are still magnificent. Crystal cool water rushes over ancient river rocks; little paths wind through native forests of hardwood, evergreen, and pine; endless ridgelines tower over valleys covered in mist; rhododendrons bloom full and large; and the soft fragrance of the mountain laurel gives this old, isolated world its special magic. The beauty of this place defies description. Flowers bloom and eagles soar over a lush green landscape that engulfs and welcomes you. There is an ancient soul to this place that says, "Come, sit and renew your spirit. Time will wait."

My place, in the midst of this abundance of nature, is back in a mountain hollow on a bad dirt road surrounded by forest, wild blackberries, mountain critters, wildflowers, a few neighbors, and a passel of "dawgs." The wild animals who live here feel safe enough to wander in the daytime, and I never cease to be thrilled by the wild turkeys walking about with their young. Red foxes dart about and, in the spring and summer, cottontail bunnies appear in my garden and can be seen following one another up and down the road. I once saw a beaver down the road a ways, exploring a large pile of newly cut trees. He looked up as I drove by and was so close that I could see the pattern on his tail. Raccoons and possums come out at night.

On a late summer day, Rosie, my dawg, was chasing a rabbit that had gotten into the garden, and both of them disappeared down the mountain. A slight wind had cooled the lazy afternoon and

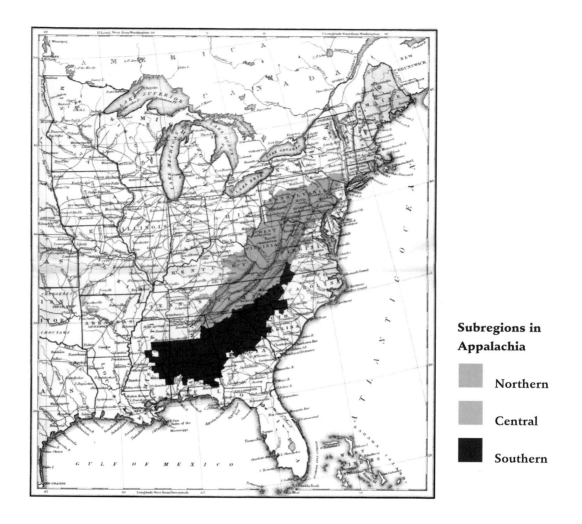

Subregions in Appalachia

Northern

Central

Southern

brought a flock of geese. The crows that nest at the top of the old maple tree were having a lively conversation and I was sitting on the back deck of the cabin, looking out over the great expanse of mountains. I couldn't help but feel a little wistful for the past and fretful about the future of this beautiful and peaceful place. The modern world is coming in full force, and the place I've come to love is steadily changing. Some folks here call it

an invasion; some call it progress. Either way, the transformation is well under way and there's no stopping it. Farm fields where I once photographed a wonderful variety of horses and old barns are gone and small residential developments have taken their place. An overabundance of tourist cabins dots the landscape and the traffic that brings so many to this place is also having an effect. It's a double-edged sword. On the one hand, the people of the region need "outside" resources, but on the other hand, these resources will continue to alter this ancient culture. In writing this book, I hope to share some of what I am lucky enough to experience day by day: the place, the people, the food, and the constant feeling of peace.

Southern Appalachia is made up of sections of eight states, and while there are major cities and a variety of socio-economic conditions, I wanted to capture a more rural aspect of the area in this book. After all, that's what makes up most of this vast and beautiful region. There is so much national and local history here and so much territory to cover that the book can represent only a small sampling of the area, its people, its stories, and its delicious food.

To really get to know a place, you have to learn a little about the people who built it, so I've included some histories about the people of the region. Southern Appalachia is like any other place. There's the part visitors see and the part that belongs to the locals. People are born, get educated, go to work, worship, and hold dear those traditions that make them special. So much has been written about the area that visitors come here expecting to see Ma and Pa Kettle of movie fame, sittin' in bare feet on the front stoop, smoking corncob pipes, with a passel of unkempt "young'uns" running all over the place. I've seen folks sitting together on the front porch after Sunday supper and I've seen well-dressed families going to church and then out to eat, but I've yet to run into Ma and Pa Kettle. The people of southern Appalachia, many of whom can trace their ancestors in this place back to the early 1600s, are as unique as the mountains where they live. Tough, resilient, reverent, proud, hardworking, and patriotic, they represent a continuation of that spirit of the early settlers who struggled and built a life of freedom and purpose. Far from the unfortunate stereotypes often seen by outsiders, mountain folks are to be admired. I hope I've captured that.

In this book, you will find old recipes dating back to the 1800s, time-tested and award-winning recipes, and more contemporary recipes from many of the bed-and-breakfast inns that dot the southern Appalachians. It's my opinion that all cultures that make up a region should be honored for their contributions, and in that spirit you will find many Cherokee recipes, African-American recipes, and Melungeon recipes, along with recipes from the Europeans who settled in the region. Many friends and neighbors here have graciously shared their family recipes with me, and I've come upon quite a few of my own favorites over the years. I hope you enjoy making these recipes as much as I do, and I hope they give you a little taste of southern Appalachia. Enjoy!

chapter 1

SOUTHERN APPALACHIA

FIVE HUNDRED AND FORTY TWO MILLION YEARS AGO, during the Paleozoic era, a great collision between the continent of the future North America and the continent of the future Africa caused the land to fold upward, creating the Appalachian Mountains. Stretching from Canada to Alabama, the Appalachians are the oldest mountain range on the American continent. This set the stage for the lush and bountiful area now known as southern Appalachia.

———✦———

Imagine a tropical climate with cloudy, mist-covered mountains and valleys awakening each day to the seasons of the sun. Eons go by and the forests become thick and home to birds and animals. Mountain rivers and streams flow with water so clear and clean that the rocks beneath glisten in the sun. Untouched and perfect, this land from the beginning of time stood silently as the winds blew and the seasons passed, and then, about 14,000 years ago, man came into this place.

Native peoples, who would later be known as the Cherokee, came into the southern regions of this ancient and lush land. They called it Shaconage, meaning "blue like smoke" after the smoke-like fogs that rise from the mountains. For thousands of years, the Cherokee cultivated the area and made the southern Appalachians their homeland. Their ancient culture was interrupted in 1539 with the coming of the Spanish and Hernando de Soto. Time and circumstance have seen ancient explorers, pirates, adventurers, wars, and people looking for freedom come into the region. Isolated from the outside world and understood by only a few, the southern Appalachian Mountains would be crisscrossed for centuries by these "invaders."

Long before the Europeans crossed over into the area, three main groups called the mountains their home. The Cherokee, the Melungeons, and the black Africans were living in peace and relative prosperity when the Europeans arrived. Their cultures, though independent of each other, traded with and assisted each other when needed. In the 1700s the first European settlers to the region emigrated from previously settled areas in the American colonies: Germans and Scotch-Irish from Pennsylvania, English from the eastern sections of Virginia and the Carolinas, and Scandinavians from the Delaware Valley. This wonderful blending of cultures, traditions, and foods is what gives southern Appalachia its unique flavor.

"The sons and daughters of the pioneers of Appalachia abounded in gentleness, kindness, and compassion; and were without pretentiousness. I think those were their prominent, and, of course, most admirable traits. They were also imaginative, resourceful, and possessed of much native acumen."

—John Rice Irwin, founder, Museum of Appalachia

FIRST SETTLERS IN THE REGION: TSA-LA-GI—THE CHEROKEE

The Cherokee call themselves *Ani-Yun-Wiya*, the principal people. They're also known as the *Ani-Kituhwagi*, the people of Kituhwa, an ancient city located near present-day Bryson City, North Carolina, which was the center of the Cherokee nation. Part of the Iroquoian lineage, the Cherokee arrived in the southeast after leaving the Great Lakes region of North America. Cherokee lands covered 40,000 square miles of southern Appalachia, and the Cherokee enjoyed a prosperous life.

Cherokee villages were built along riverbanks and connected by a series of roads. Each village had a council house, and each council house had seven sides representing the seven clans of the Cherokee. The door faced east toward the rising sun and there was a sacred fire burning in the center of the floor. A Cherokee village consisted of about fifty log homes built around a central area where the council house was located.

Women were the heads of households, with the home and the children belonging to her should she separate from or lose her husband. In the matriarchal society, membership in a clan came through the mother. When a child was born, he or she became a member of the mother's clan. Once a couple married, they lived with the wife's clan. It was the wife's male relatives rather than the father who typically disciplined and taught the children. The father's clan was allowed to name the children. If a woman's husband failed to please her, was unfaithful, or disgraced her clan, she could divorce him by simply placing a deerskin outside of their dwelling and placing his belongings on it. He was then expected to leave.

After de Soto "discovered" the Cherokee in 1540, life would never be the same. By the 1600s not only the Spanish but also the French and English traders were on Cherokee land. From the early 1700s to the Revolutionary War, the tribe found itself in constant conflict with colonial armies.

The Cherokee provided food for the new settlers and showed them how to survive, but the European colonists thought of them as savages. Nothing was further from the truth. The Cherokee were a highly ordered society. They built roads, schools, and churches; had a system of representative government; and were farmers and cattle ranchers. They lived in log homes, some two stories high, and wore European-style clothing. War and European diseases decimated the tribe, and in 1738, smallpox eliminated one-quarter of the Cherokee nation. The Cherokee were eventually forced to sign over most of their land, first to the British and then to the United States. In 1827, the Cherokee wrote a constitution and declared themselves a sovereign nation.

Upon learning that gold had been found on Cherokee lands, President Andrew Jackson passed into law the Indian Removal Act of 1830 and set the stage for the complete devastation of the Cherokee people. In 1838, President Martin Van Buren appointed General Winfield Scott to lead the forcible removal operation. Commanding some 7,000 troops, Scott arrived in Georgia on May 26 and began a forcible evacuation at gunpoint. There was no warning. Men and women were working in the fields and children were with grandparents or friends when the troops arrived and herded the Cherokee into makeshift forts, where they were held against their will. The

Cherokee nation was forced to give up its lands east of the Mississippi River and walk to an area in present-day Oklahoma. People call this journey the "Trail of Tears" because of its devastating effects. Trail "Where They Cried" (*nu na hi du na tlo hi lu i*, the Cherokee name), a 2,200-mile trek that killed more than 4,000 Cherokees, was one of the cruelest crimes committed by a government against its people.

A few Cherokees, refusing to move, hid in the wilderness of the Great Smoky Mountains. Avoiding the authorities, these Cherokees, now called the Eastern Band, were allowed to claim some of their lands in western North Carolina in the 1870s. In 1889, this 56,000-acre section of land was chartered and is now called the Qualla Boundary, home to almost 11,000 descendents of the original Cherokee nation. Far from having the devastation found on many reservations, the Qualla Boundary is a beautiful place.

The Cherokee were and are an accomplished people. George Gist, known to the world as Sequoyah, invented the Cherokee Syllabary, which has been called "unrivaled in all human history." The syllabary freed the Cherokee from the bonds of illiteracy. The alphabet was adopted by the Cherokee Nation in 1821, and shortly after, the Cherokee newspaper was created.

Cherokee women traditionally raised crops of corn, beans, squash, and sunflowers. These were preserved and saved for winter. They gathered wild fruits like persimmon and mulberry and made bread from dried persimmon flour. Hickory nuts were gathered and the meats removed and added to water, making a drink called hickory milk, or *ganu gwala sti.*

By the late 1700s, Cherokee women had added several new foods to their gardens. Watermelon, an African plant, had been adopted by the Spanish and was brought to the region in the 1500s. Peach trees were also brought to the region by the Spanish. Peaches (*khwa na*) were pounded and mixed with flour to make bread, cooked and dried for winter storage, and used to flavor their delicious soups and beverages. The Cherokee also raised hogs and cattle and fished.

Be sure to try John Cripe's Fry Bread on page 186. He has served this to me many times and it's always a treat. I've eaten a lot of fry bread at Native American powwows and gatherings, but his is my favorite. Pepper Pot Soup on page 156 is another traditional and delicious recipe, just perfect when you're feeling like a hearty bowl of soup.

SECOND SETTLERS IN THE REGION: THE MELUNGEONS

A few generations ago, children in Tennessee, Virginia, and surrounding areas were told, "If you don't behave, the Melungeons will get you!" Many people grew up believing the Melungeons were an Appalachian version of the boogeyman, a myth. They were no myth. They are considered one of world's greatest anthropological mysteries, a tribe of "natives" twice discovered in the Appalachian Mountains prior to early European settlement of the region.

To date, the origin of the Melungeons remains clouded in mystery. However, Dr. Brent Kennedy, a Melungeon himself, has done extensive research into his own origins and has opened up the entire field of Melungeon research. In his book *The Melungeons: The Resurrection of a Proud People*, cowritten with Robyn Vaughan Kennedy, Kennedy speaks to the Spanish Inquisition and how he feels that "there is little doubt that the Inquisition—with all its agonies—drove Spanish and Portuguese Muslims toward the New World." In 1566, the Spanish established the colony Santa Elena in South Carolina. According to Kennedy, "Many of the Santa Elena colonists were Berber Muslims and Sephardic Jews, recruited by the Portuguese Captain Joao Pardo from the heavily Berber Galician Mountains of northern Portugal in 1567." When Santa Elena fell to the British in 1587, its inhabitants, including the converted Jews and Muslims, escaped into the mountains of North Carolina. Kennedy goes on to say, "In the 1690s, French explorers reported finding 'Christianized Moors' in the Carolina mountains. When the first English arrived in the mid 1700s, large colonies of so-called 'Melungeons' were already well established in the Tennessee and Carolina mountains. And, in broken Elizabethan English they called themselves 'Portyghee,' or by the more mysterious term 'Melungeon.'"

According to Kennedy, "Over years, as growing numbers of Anglo settlers swept upon them and around them, Melungeons were pushed higher and higher into the mountains. And their claims of Portuguese and Melungeon heritage were increasingly ridiculed. Even the word Melungeon became a most disparaging term. In fact, to be legally classified as a Melungeon meant in the words of one journalist, to be 'nobody at all.' The Melungeons, pushed off their lands, denied their rights, often murdered, always mistreated, became an embittered and nearly defeated people. Over the ensuing decades, in a vain effort to fit in with their Anglo neighbors, they lost their heritage, their culture, the names and their original religion but not their genetic structure."

Melungeons identified themselves with Anglo surnames like Goins, Mullins, and Collins. They possessed no written record and passed their history down by the tradition of storytelling. Some of the Melungeons in east Tennessee came to take up land grants shortly after the Revolutionary War. They settled in the Vardy Valley, named for Melungeon Vardiman Collins, close to Newman's

Ridge. A narrow valley between Powell Mountain and Newman's Ridge just north of Sneedville, Tennessee, and the county seat of Hancock County, Vardy is the traditional home of the Melungeons. Like most mountain people, they were self-sufficient and possessed remarkable skills. They were expert miners and gifted silversmiths, and they survived by minting their own coinage.

Because of their racial classification as nonwhite, employment was rare and Melungeons often had to stay alive by engaging in making moonshine and other various "underground activities." One such person was Mahala Mullens, born in 1824 in Hancock County, Tennessee. She is also known as "Big Haley" and "Aunt Haley," and was probably the most famous Melungeon in the Newman's Ridge area. Aunt Haley openly sold moonshine in her log house high on Newman's Ridge. The poor woman was a victim of elephantiasis and weighed more than 400 pounds. She was too large to be taken out of the house if the authorities tried to arrest her. One deputy reportedly told the sheriff, "She's catchable, but not fetchable." An 1897 article, "Visit to the Melungeons," by C. H. Humble was published in the *Home Mission Monthly*. It describes Aunt Haley: "The most noted person now among them is Mrs. Mehala Mullens, widow of John Mullens. About twenty children were born to this couple, three of whom met violent deaths, one son being shot in the streets of Sneedville, another in her door yard, and a third lynched in Texas." He goes on to say, "I asked what she was going to do with all the fruit in the large orchard? She replied, 'The boys know how to work that up.' I presumed into apple brandy, and she will do the rest."

Mahala Mullens died in 1898. It's said that a wall had to be removed to get her out of the house and that her bed had to be made into a casket. She is buried next to her cabin. When Aunt Haley died, her obituary ran in newspapers across the country.

Since their arrival on this continent, Melungeons have intermarried with native tribes, black Africans, and Europeans. They are classified as "tri-racial" people, and many modern-day Melungeons, like Kennedy, are actively researching their heritage.

When Melungeons first came to the Appalachians, the foods they ate were the same as those eaten by native tribes. An old recipe for Cherokee Sweet Bread, called *oo-ga-na-s-diga-do*, is one

example. They also ate wild tangle gut greens and pusley, as well as scrapple, which was made from boiled hog's head. The Europeans who came later to the mountains also ate scrapple. Along with recipes for corn, beans, and chicken, I've found recipes for groundhog patties, and one for rabbit. I asked an old-timer about eating groundhog, who laughed and told me that it's quite delicious. Apparently the groundhog is a vegetarian, and so the meat is considered clean and healthy. I've found Melungeon dessert recipes that are more than one hundred years old. I've shared many of these recipes in this book, including one for Cranberry Cream Pie on page 153, which has become a favorite at my Thanksgiving dinner.

THIRD SETTLERS IN THE REGION: THE BLACK AFRICANS

Although there is evidence placing black Africans on the continent for thousands of years, blacks and Moors were first recorded in the Appalachian Mountains in the 1300s. Early Spanish and French explorers brought African slaves and free persons of color with them and many stayed behind. Life for these early Moorish and African settlers was possibly easier than it was for the Europeans. The blacks and Moors intermingled with the Cherokee and Melungeons and in many cases married into these other cultures. They enjoyed freedom and the benefits of the ordered Cherokee society. This all changed with the coming of slavery.

In 1619, the first Africans arrived in Jamestown, Virginia, as indentured servants. By 1641, laws had made them legal chattel slaves who could be bought and solely owned by their masters, thus formalizing slavery. In 1775, 5,000 African-

Americans served under George Washington in the Revolutionary War. During the ensuing years, runaway slaves and freedmen of color escaped into the southern Appalachian Mountains and in many cases were adopted into the Cherokee tribe.

Europeans brought their slaves with them into the mountains. Slavery there was more violent than it was in larger slave populations. Appalachian farmers were not wealthy and many Appalachian plantations, though there weren't many, were small, averaging about nine slaves per farm. The selling of slaves became a source of income. In most cases, male slaves were rented out to work in hotels, mining camps, and general stores. Only about half of enslaved children lived to the age of fifteen. Those who did survive were sold away from their parents. Women were subject to continuous assault and the resulting offspring sold. Slave cabins, many of which can still be seen, were one-room places, about 16 by 16 feet with no window and a hanging cloth for a door. In more prosperous homes a fireplace was added.

After the Civil War, many blacks were homeless. Some went north, many stayed on their masters' farms, and many stayed in the area to find a place of their own. The descendants of these slaves still live and work in southern Appalachia. Non-slave African-American settlements have also existed in Appalachia since earlier times. One community, Texana, was established around 1850. Located high on a mountain in western North Carolina, Texana was named for Texas "Texana" McClelland, whose family founded the first black settlement in the area. Today the community has about 150 residents who live along the same hillside as the original inhabitants.

Despite a troubled and often violent history in the South, African-Americans have had an enormous positive impact on the culture of southern Appalachia, from their traditions to their music to their food. European slave traders, urged by their African counterparts, brought African foods over for trade in order to help the slaves settle into their new home. Yams, okra, cucumbers, black-eyed peas, rice, watermelon, seeds, and nuts all became common southern American crops, and these crops still play a huge part in the food culture of the South today. Red Beans and Rice (page 81) and Sweet and Sour Cucumbers (page 190) are traditional favorites, and I've also included some newer soul food recipes, such as Imperial Crab Balls (page 141) and Broccoli Salad, Southern-Style (page 65). And of course there's that favorite southern dish: Southern Butter-Crusted Fried Chicken (page 113).

"We have good reason to be proud of the early pioneers from Ireland and Germany, others of English, Welsh, and Scottish descent. They laid the foundations of their homes. They were men and women who suffered from conscience sake, or fled from despotism to seek liberty unrestrained by the shackles of a worn-out civilization."

—Reverend Jethro Rumple, nineteenth-century American historian

FOURTH SETTLERS IN THE REGION: THE EUROPEANS

The first European settlers to the southern highlands emigrated from previously settled areas in the United States. The Germans and Scotch-Irish came from Pennsylvania, the English from the eastern sections of Virginia and the Carolinas, and the Scandinavians from the Delaware Valley. The Scotch-Irish and Germans were the first northern Europeans to enter the southern Appalachian mountains, and their culture would become the dominant culture of the region up until the present day.

Although early American colonists knew of the Appalachian Mountains, 200 miles inland from the Atlantic coast, they did not attempt to cross them until about 150 years after the founding of Jamestown, Virginia. Born in 1734 in Pennsylvania, Daniel Boone became one of the best-known long hunters, exploring the mountains and valleys of what had become known as the "first western frontier." As word circulated about the new, abundant, and lush lands, people started to think about moving west. In September 1773 Boone led a group of settlers, including many of his in-laws, through the Cumberland Gap and into Kentucky. They were soon followed by settlers who began to take the Ohio River west to the Warrior's Path, which led them south into the interior. In 1775, an Irishman named Richard Henderson and his Transylvania Company purchased modern-day Kentucky from the Cherokee Indians. In 1785, as the young country was taking form, the three million citizens of the new nation were hearing about the rich land available at little cost.

Contact between Native Americans and the European settlers was mostly, though not always, one of conflict. This conflict was due to the natives' feeling invaded by the new settlers and a sense of superiority on the part of the Europeans, who saw no problem in settling without permission on native lands. The Europeans often saw themselves as being on a mission to conquer nature: a manifest destiny. Out of ignorance, they often viewed Native American societies as hopelessly primitive and savage and did not hesitate to use force if they felt the natives were in their way.

Deep within the mountain hollows (pronounced "hollers") the settlers staked their claims. The forests provided building materials for their log cabins and furniture. They raised small crops of corn, potatoes, black-eyed peas, fruit trees, and gourds to make containers. When the Europeans first arrived, woodland bison (buffalo) were still plentiful in what is now middle Tennessee and into the forests of the upper Tennessee Valley. The Cherokee made many delicious dishes using the meat and shared them with the new settlers. Buffalo-stuffed pumpkins and buffalo steaks were hearty fall and wintertime foods. The European men hunted the woods day and night for "beasties" with the help of their loyal dogs. (The dog—pronounced "dawg"—is still a loyal companion in the hills.) By 1800, woodland bison had become rare. Within two decades they were extinct.

The Europeans' diet consisted of corn, wild game birds, deer, bear, and elk. Many small critters like raccoon, possum, squirrel, and groundhog supplemented larger game killed on hunting trips. Wild turkey, geese, and fish are plentiful in the area to this day. One of my favorite sights is watching wild turkey families walking along my dirt road in springtime. They usually have two or three chicks with them and the parents seem to be showing them where to find food. Wild game is bountiful in the mountains, and when the settlers arrived it was even more so.

Early settlers learned how to make hominy from the Cherokee. Corn was the easiest crop to grow in the mountains. Potatoes and onions were also easy to grow. Breads were made from corn or potato meal. Berries and fruits were gathered in the wild until the settlers could transplant them. If they had a cow or goat, they made butter in a churn; however, lard, animal fat, was the ingredient most often used in cooking. Wild greens and roots, like burdock, pusley, dandelion, poke salat, and wild carrot, provided the vegetable or salad to the meal.

Nature's bounty, time-honored traditional cooking from Europe, and methods taught by native residents made survival in this isolated place possible. A mountain woman could make crops last all year long. Food was "put up" or preserved and kept in the springhouse for later use. A springhouse looks a lot like an outhouse to an "outsider." It's a small, one-room building sitting over the water of a spring. The water maintains a constant cool temperature in the building, and the foods stored inside the springhouse last longer. Springhouses can still be seen in the mountains. You may not have a springhouse, but you can still make your own preserves using the recipes in the Country Store chapter. It includes some of my favorite traditional Appalachian preserves, such as Dandelion Jelly and Blueberry Marmalade. If you like pickles, Grandma's Fresh Table Pickles are quick, easy, and delicious. And the strawberry, blackberry, pecan, and cinnamon syrups are a great way to top your pancakes, ice cream, puddings, cobblers, and pound cakes. As a matter of fact, I've known folks who like a little syrup on their biscuits.

chapter 2

BREAKFAST

EGG CASSEROLE WITH TATERS AND SAUSAGE

serves 8

LOCATED IN THE MOUNTAINS of northern Georgia, Henson Cove Bed & Breakfast in Hiawassee is a unique farmhouse-style B & B reminiscent of earlier times when fun was a trip to the mountains and nature was the entertainment. Stunning views, porch swings and rockers, exploring, and fun activities give you a real country appetite. This breakfast casserole, which you prepare the night before and refrigerate overnight, is hearty and delicious and will hold you over through lunch. You can cut the recipe in half (using 6 eggs) for an 8- or 9-inch square pan.

1 pound breakfast sausage (preferably Jimmy Dean)

½ medium yellow onion, finely chopped

3 cups cold cooked potatoes cut into small cubes

1 (4-ounce) can diced green chilies

1 cup low-fat small-curd cottage cheese

1 to 2 cups grated cheddar cheese

10 to 12 large eggs, lightly beaten

1 teaspoon salt

¼ teaspoon freshly ground black pepper

Pinch of nutmeg

Fresh cilantro leaves, for garnish

Chopped tomato, for garnish

Salsa, for serving

GREASE a 9 by 13-inch baking dish. In a skillet over medium heat, combine the sausage and onion and cook until the sausage is browned.

IN A LARGE BOWL, combine the potatoes, chilies, cottage cheese, cheddar, eggs, salt, pepper, and nutmeg. Stir to blend. Add the cooked sausage mixture and blend. Pour into the prepared baking dish, cover, and refrigerate overnight.

IN THE MORNING, preheat the oven to 350°F. Bake for 1 hour, or until set. Garnish with cilantro and tomato and serve with salsa on the side.

OATMEAL–BROWN SUGAR PANCAKES

serves 4 to 5

THE PROSPECT HILL BED & BREAKFAST INN is an 1889 Victorian country mansion in Mountain City, Tennessee, with quick access to the southwest Virginia highlands and North Carolina's high country. These pancakes are easy and delicious. Serve them with some Tennessee bacon on the side for a full and filling breakfast.

---

1 large egg

1 cup milk

2 tablespoons vegetable oil

1 cup all-purpose flour

1 teaspoon baking powder

½ teaspoon baking soda

½ teaspoon salt

¼ cup firmly packed brown sugar

½ cup quick-cooking oats

BEAT the egg in a large bowl. Add the milk and oil and mix well. In a medium bowl, combine the flour, baking powder, baking soda, salt, and brown sugar. Add the dry mixture to the egg mixture, mixing until blended. Add the oats and blend well.

HEAT a lightly greased griddle over medium heat. For each pancake, pour about ¼ cup batter onto the griddle, allowing room for the batter to spread and not touch other pancakes. Flip the pancakes when the tops are covered with bubbles and the edges look cooked, and cook until browned on both sides. Serve immediately.

Tennessee Bacon

makes 1 pound

If you've never made bacon like this, you are in for a treat!

½ cup all-purpose flour

¼ cup firmly packed brown sugar

1 teaspoon freshly ground black pepper

1 pound sliced country-style bacon

HEAT a skillet over medium-high heat or preheat the oven to 400°F. Sift together the flour, sugar, and pepper. Dredge the bacon in the flour to coat it evenly. Pan-fry the bacon in the skillet or bake it in the oven until brown and crisp.

OVEN-BAKED BLUEBERRY FRENCH TOAST

serves 5

THIS RECIPE, FROM the Cripple Creek Bed and Breakfast Cabins in Crockett, Virginia, was handed down from the owner's grandmother. Cripple Creek is situated in the Blue Ridge Mountains on 35 acres of wooded hills and rolling pastures dotted with wildflowers, blackberry bushes, and apple trees. I just love blueberries, so I hope this recipe from Cripple Creek will become one of your favorites!

2 (8-ounce) packages cream cheese, at room temperature

½ cup granulated sugar

2 teaspoons vanilla extract

1 teaspoon ground cinnamon

2 large eggs

1½ cups milk

10 slices French bread, ¾ inch thick (preferably homemade or fresh store-bought)

2 cups fresh blueberries

Maple syrup, for serving

Confectioners' sugar, for serving

PREHEAT the oven to 350°F and lightly grease a 9 by 13-inch baking dish. Beat the cream cheese, granulated sugar, vanilla, and cinnamon in a large bowl with a stand mixer on medium speed until well blended. Add the eggs, one at a time, mixing well after each addition. Add the milk and mix well.

ARRANGE the bread in the prepared baking dish and spread the blueberries on top of the bread. Pour the cream cheese mixture over the bread. Let stand for at least 15 minutes before baking (or cover the pan and place it in the refrigerator overnight). Bake for 40 to 45 minutes, until golden brown. Serve with maple syrup and confectioners' sugar.

THREE-CHEESE SOUFFLÉ

serves 2

BUILT IN THE LATE 1920S, the Buttonwood Inn in Franklin, North Carolina, is full of charming antiques, collectibles, handmade family quilts, and country pieces that make you feel like you're staying in a true southern Appalachian family home. Whether you want to enjoy mountain views from a rocking chair on the deck or prefer to try some white-water rafting, you can awaken in the morning to this wonderful breakfast soufflé.

2 large eggs, separated, whites at room temperature

1 tablespoon sour cream

1 teaspoon water

½ teaspoon baking powder

½ teaspoon mixed herbs (fresh if available: basil, thyme, parsley, and oregano)

4 to 5 dashes of hot sauce

⅛ cup grated Swiss cheese

⅛ cup grated cheddar cheese

⅛ cup grated Monterey Jack cheese

PREHEAT the oven to 350°F. Grease two 6-ounce soufflé cups thoroughly. Beat the egg whites to stiff peaks and set aside.

PUT the egg yolks in a medium bowl and add the sour cream, water, baking powder, herbs, and hot sauce, stirring well. Fold the egg whites and the cheeses into the egg yolk mixture. Pour into the prepared soufflé cups. Bake for 12 to 14 minutes, until fluffy and brown. Serve hot.

appalachian phrases

"Well bless her heart": anything from truly "bless her heart" to "what a pity she's so odd."

"Which one of them gals is the bell cow?": Which one, in the group of ladies, is the leader?

"How's ya momma 'n 'em?": How's your family?

"Beetle-browed": has brows that hang over.

"Don't go back on your raisin'": Never deny your heritage.

"He's all hat and no cattle": He's all talk.

SHIRRED EGGS

serves as many as you need to feed

A FAVORITE RETREAT FOR ARTISTS AND WRITERS, the Farmhouse Inn at Good Spring Farm in Parkers Lake, Kentucky, was built in the early 1920s. Good Spring Farm, a Kentucky Centennial Farm, has been owned and farmed by the Taylor family for more than one hundred years. It's surrounded by the natural beauty of the Daniel Boone National Forest. The Farmhouse Inn serves organic food, and their shirred eggs are best when you start with fresh organic or free-range eggs.

FOR EACH PERSON, YOU'LL NEED:

1 slice ham

½ cup plus ¼ cup shredded cheddar, Monterey Jack,
    Colby, or Mexican blend cheese

1 or 2 large eggs

3 tablespoons half-and-half

Coarsely ground black pepper

Dried red pepper flakes

1 English muffin

Fresh parsley, for garnish

PREHEAT the oven to 375°F and lightly coat individual ovenproof baking dishes with nonstick cooking spray. Place 1 ham slice on the bottom of each dish and top with ½ cup of the shredded cheese to make a nest. Crack the egg into the cheese nest and pour the half-and-half over the top. Sprinkle the remaining ¼ cup cheese over the egg. Sprinkle the black pepper and dried red pepper flakes over the top.

PLACE the baking dishes on a baking sheet and bake for 20 minutes, or until golden and the egg whites are set. To serve, slice the English muffin in half, toast it, top it with the shirred egg, and garnish with the parsley.

HIGH COUNTRY BREAKFAST CASSEROLE

serves 6

THE BUFFALO TAVERN BED AND BREAKFAST in West Jefferson, North Carolina, is a landmark from the days when horse-drawn wagons traveled the roads of Ashe County. Built around 1872, it still greets visitors today. People in the area know it as the "large white house on Buffalo Road." Prep this breakfast casserole the night before serving and you'll have a fast, easy, and delicious breakfast in the morning.

———————

1 pound ground sausage

1 loaf French bread, cut into 1-inch cubes

1 cup shredded Colby cheese

1 cup shredded Monterey Jack cheese

12 large eggs

3 cups plus ½ soup can (see below) cold milk

1 teaspoon dry mustard

1 (10½-ounce) can mushroom soup

Sliced tomatoes, for serving

IN A LARGE SKILLET over medium heat, cook the sausage. Drain off excess drippings.

LIGHTLY coat an 8 by 13-inch glass baking dish with nonstick cooking spray and line the bottom of the dish with the cubed bread. Spread the cooked sausage over the bread cubes and sprinkle the cheeses over the top.

PLACE the eggs in a large bowl and slowly whisk in 3 cups of the cold milk until blended. Whisk in the dry mustard. Pour the egg mixture over the top of the cheese. Cover the dish with aluminum foil and refrigerate overnight.

IN THE MORNING, preheat the oven to 325°F. In a small bowl, combine the mushroom soup and remaining ½ soup can of milk. Blend well. Pour over the top of the casserole, covering everything. Bake for 1 hour and 15 minutes, or until set. Cut into squares and serve with sliced tomatoes on the side.

STRAWBERRY-BANANA PANCAKES

serves 7 to 8

THE BRADY INN BED AND BREAKFAST is in the historic district of Madison, Georgia. It's full of old-fashioned charm and true Southern hospitality. These pancakes are as good as they sound. You might want to add a side of bacon or sausage patties to the plate or more fruit on the side.

2 cups all-purpose flour

2 teaspoons baking powder

½ teaspoon baking soda

½ teaspoon salt

¼ cup granulated sugar

4 large eggs

1¾ cups buttermilk

4 tablespoons (½ stick) unsalted butter, melted and
   cooled

Canola oil

½ cup mashed ripe bananas

½ cup diced fresh strawberries, plus strawberry halves
   for garnish

Confectioners' sugar, for dusting

Maple syrup, for serving

MIX the flour, baking powder, baking soda, salt, and granulated sugar together in a large bowl. In a medium bowl, blend the eggs, buttermilk, and melted butter. Pour the liquid mixture into the center of the dry mixture and blend by hand just until evenly moistened.

HEAT a griddle over medium high heat for about 5 minutes. Use a paper towel to wipe the surface with a thin layer of canola oil.

FOLD the bananas and strawberries into the batter. Drop a little less than ¼ cup of batter for each pancake onto the griddle, allowing room for the batter to spread and not touch other pancakes. Cook until small bubbles appear on the top surface, about 2 minutes. Turn the pancakes over and cook for another 1 to 2 minutes, until golden brown.

TO SERVE, overlap three pancakes across each plate. Dust with confectioners' sugar and drizzle with maple syrup. Garnish with strawberry halves.

CRUSTLESS TOMATO PIE

serves 12 to 18

KNOWN FOR ITS ART AND MUSIC WORKSHOPS, musical performances, and catering, the Mentone Inn in Mentone, Alabama, is a historic part of the area. This tomato pie is the signature dish at the inn. When fresh tomatoes aren't available, substitute diced tomatoes. You can use the tomato mixture immediately, but allowing it to marinate overnight intensifies the flavor.

---

12 ripe Roma tomatoes, or 1½ to 2 (14½-ounce) cans
    diced tomatoes

¼ cup balsamic vinegar

¼ cup olive oil

2 teaspoons Greek seasoning

12 medium eggs, beaten

1 teaspoon salt

1 teaspoon freshly ground black pepper

1½ cups shredded cheddar cheese

1½ cups shredded mozzarella cheese

1 cup mayonnaise

SLICE the tomatoes crosswise into ¼-inch-thick slices and put them in a large bowl. Add the vinegar and oil and toss to coat. Add 1 teaspoon of Greek seasoning and mix well. Cover and refrigerate the mixture overnight.

PREHEAT the oven to 350°F. Lightly coat a 9 by 13-inch baking dish with nonstick cooking spray. Pour the tomato mixture into the prepared dish and spread evenly. Add the eggs to the empty tomato bowl and beat well. Add the salt and pepper and ½ teaspoon of Greek seasoning. Pour the mixture evenly over the tomatoes.

IN A MEDIUM BOWL, mix the cheddar and mozzarella cheeses together. Add the mayonnaise and stir to make a paste. Spread evenly over the egg and tomato mixture and sprinkle the remaining ½ teaspoon of Greek seasoning over the top.

BAKE for 30 to 45 minutes, until the eggs are set. Let stand for 10 minutes before cutting into squares and serving.

PANCAKES SUZETTE

serves 4

FLO'S HIDEAWAY in the historic town of Bristol, Virginia, is in the middle of the historic district on Solar Hill. It's got plenty of southern hospitality with a European twist, thanks to French-born and -raised hostess Flo. Whether you are in Bristol for a NASCAR event or to explore the true home of country music, the Flo's Hideaway Pancakes Suzette are a delightful way to start your day.

---

4 servings of your favorite pancake mix, prepared according to package directions

4 tablespoons (½ stick) unsalted butter

1 cup sugar

1½ cups orange juice

2 tablespoons Grand Marnier (optional)

Juice of 1 lemon

Curls of fresh orange zest, for serving

Curls of fresh lemon zest, for serving

Fresh mint leaves, for serving

KEEP the cooked pancakes warm by either tenting them with aluminum foil or placing them in a warm oven while you make the sauce.

IN A SAUCEPAN over medium-low heat, combine the butter and sugar. Cook until the sugar is dissolved and the mixture is smooth, stirring constantly so that it doesn't burn. Add the orange juice, Grand Marnier, and lemon juice. Stirring constantly, let the mixture cook until it becomes a light syrup. Do not overcook.

TO SERVE, arrange warm pancakes on a plate and pour some hot syrup over them. Garnish with orange and lemon zest and mint. Bon appétit!

CRUNCHY, NUTTY, STUFFED FRENCH TOAST

serves 6 to 12

THIS RECIPE FROM THE HIDDEN VALLEY BED & BREAKFAST, in Hiawassee, Georgia, is yummy! The inn is a charming place with lovely rooms and so serene that's it's hard to imagine that civilization is nearby. This recipe is so good, but I also invite you to experiment with it. Instead of raspberry jam, add some crushed fresh fruit, like bananas, peaches, or berries, or even your favorite marmalade. The inn serves two pieces of French toast per person. Put any leftover cereal mix in a plastic freezer bag and freeze it for later.

1 long French baguette

1 (8-ounce) package cream cheese

⅓ (12-ounce) jar of seedless raspberry jam

4 large eggs

¼ cup half-and-half

2 to 3 cups crushed Honey Bunches of Oats cereal

Handful of chopped pecans

Handful of shredded sweetened coconut

Confectioners' sugar, for dusting (optional)

Maple syrup, for serving (optional)

PREHEAT the oven to 300°F.

SLICE the baguette diagonally into ¾-inch-thick slices almost to the crust. You should have at least twelve slices, all still attached at the bottom of the loaf. Next, cut down through the middle of each slice, again almost to the crust. You are basically making a pocket in each slice. Holding onto the loaf, spread 1 tablespoon of the cream cheese into each pocket, then spread about 2 tablespoons of jam onto the cream cheese.

LIGHTLY beat the eggs and half-and-half together in a medium bowl. In a separate bowl, mix the cereal, pecans, and coconut. Now go ahead and cut the original slices all the way through the crust so that you have twelve individual "sandwiches" with cream cheese and jam in the middle pockets. Using tongs, dip each slice into the egg mixture, making sure to coat each side of bread. Then lay each side of the bread slice into the cereal mixture, coating it heavily with cereal.

PUT a mixture of oil and butter on a large griddle and heat it over medium heat. Lay the bread slices on the griddle and cook until the cereal is toasted to a golden brown. Flip the slices and cook the other side. Transfer the slices to a baking sheet and put them in the oven for at least 30 minutes before serving. The slices can be kept warm in the oven for up to 1 hour.

TO SERVE, dust with confectioners' sugar and drizzle maple syrup over the top.

BERRY PARFAIT

serves 4

THIS RECIPE COMES FROM THE CLAIBORNE HOUSE INN in Rocky Mount, Virginia. Fresh berries are best, but frozen ones will work, too.

———◆———

½ cup muesli or granola (any variety without raisins)

I cup vanilla or strawberry yogurt

½ cup fresh or frozen raspberries or strawberries, plus more for garnish

Whipped cream, for serving

PUT a spoonful of the muesli in each of four parfait or dessert cups, and then add a spoonful of yogurt to each and top with a few berries. Repeat with another layer of muesli, yogurt, and berries. Top with a dollop of whipped cream and garnish with a few raspberries or sliced strawberries. Serve immediately.

HEAVENLY EGGS

serves 6

BUILT IN 1902 in the heart of the Smoky Mountains and lovingly restored, the Angels Landing Inn in Murphy, North Carolina, exemplifies old-fashioned Southern living with just a splash of Victorian charm. These eggs are a constant favorite with guests and easy to prepare.

———◆———

6 slices Canadian bacon

6 slices Swiss cheese

6 large eggs

I (8-ounce) carton heavy whipping cream

Parmesan cheese, for sprinkling

PREHEAT the oven to 400°F and spray the bottom of 6 individual ramekins with nonstick cooking spray. Place the ramekins on a rimmed baking sheet or in a 9 by 13-inch baking dish.

PLACE 1 slice of Canadian bacon on the bottom of each ramekin. Top with a slice of Swiss cheese. Break 1 egg over each piece of cheese, taking care to keep the yolk intact. Pour the heavy cream over the top just until the yolk pops out from the cream.

BAKE the ramekins for 10 to 12 minutes. Remove from the oven and sprinkle Parmesan cheese over the top of each serving. Return to the oven and bake for 10 to 12 minutes more, until the cheese is melted. Serve immediately.

LEMON-PEPPER POPOVERS

makes 12

THE AMBROSIA FARM BED & BREAKFAST AND POTTERY is located along Virginia's Crooked Road Historic Music Trail in the Blue Ridge Mountains of southwestern Virginia, halfway between the town of Floyd and the Blue Ridge Parkway. The inn offers summer art camps for children ages nine to sixteen and art-related activities for guests of all ages throughout the year. They also offer these delicious popovers, usually with some fresh cubed watermelon and cantaloupe sprinkled with lime juice and chopped fresh mint. Popovers are best when warm, so enjoy these right out of the oven.

1½ cups milk

½ cup water

4 large eggs, beaten

1 tablespoon fresh lemon zest

2 tablespoons unsalted butter, melted

1½ cups all-purpose flour

1 teaspoon salt

1 tablespoon freshly ground black pepper

Unsalted butter, for serving

PREHEAT the oven to 375°F. Butter a standard 12-cup muffin pan.

IN A LARGE BOWL, combine the milk, water, eggs, and lemon zest. Whisk until well combined. Whisk in the melted butter. Slowly add the flour and whisk until well blended. Add the salt and pepper and blend well.

POUR the batter into the prepared muffin pan and bake for 35 minutes, until the popovers are puffed and brown. Serve piping hot with butter.

GUTEN MORGEN EGGS

serves 4 to 6

THE CHALET INN in Dillsboro, North Carolina, is situated right where the Blue Ridge Mountains meet the Great Smoky Mountains, and it's a picture-perfect setting: forested mountain ridges with wildflowers, brook, ponds, waterfalls, and naturalized gardens. The inn's breakfast casserole is great because it's a versatile recipe that can be changed according to the season or what you have on hand. You can use Vidalia onions in the summer instead of scallions, fresh dill instead of parsley, cottage cheese instead of sour cream. You can also vary the cheese, using blue cheese, Parmesan, mozzarella, or other cheeses.

---

16 large eggs

1 teaspoon ground nutmeg

Pinch of salt

Pinch of freshly ground black pepper

1 tablespoon fresh or dried parsley

¼ cup finely chopped scallions, white parts only

½ cup sour cream

8 to 12 fresh mushrooms, sliced (optional)

2 cups grated sharp cheddar cheese

THE NIGHT BEFORE you plan to serve the eggs, lightly grease two 5 by 9 by 3-inch baking dishes. In a medium bowl, beat together the eggs, nutmeg, salt, pepper, parsley, and scallions. Cook the scrambled mixture in a skillet over medium heat.

PLACE the scrambled eggs in the bottom of the baking dishes. Spread half of the sour cream over each dish of eggs, and then top with the mushrooms and cheese. Cover and refrigerate overnight.

IN THE MORNING, preheat the oven to 325°F. Remove the baking dishes from the refrigerator and let them come to room temperature. Bake for 30 minutes. Serve hot.

APPLE-PORK BRUNCH PIE

makes one 9- or 10-inch pie

GRACE HILL INN IN TOWNSEND, TENNESSEE, sits high in the hills and offers the most spectacular views of the Great Smoky Mountains. Award after award has been presented to this extraordinary place, and I'm so thrilled they shared this recipe with me. Their brunch pie is a delicious combination of sweet and savory flavors. It's also very easy. You can prepare the crust and filling ahead of time and refrigerate until ready to use. Once assembled, the pie can be baked immediately or frozen and baked later.

CRUST

8 ounces lard or vegetable shortening

3 cups all-purpose flour

1 teaspoon salt

Cold milk, as needed

FILLING

½ cup granulated sugar

½ cup firmly packed brown sugar

⅓ cup all-purpose flour

1 teaspoon ground cinnamon

¼ teaspoon ground nutmeg

2 to 3 Granny Smith apples, peeled, cored, and thinly sliced

1 (1 pound) package bulk pork sausage

½ cup chopped white onion

1 egg yolk, beaten, for brushing

PREHEAT the oven to 425°F.

TO MAKE THE CRUST, place the lard in a large bowl and cut in the flour and salt using a pastry blender or a fork. With a fork, stir in enough cold milk to form a ball in the center of the bowl. Divide the ball in half. Roll out one half on a floured surface until it is about 12 inches in diameter and transfer to the bottom of a pie pan.

TO MAKE THE FILLING, mix the granulated sugar, brown sugar, flour, cinnamon, and nutmeg in a large bowl. Add the apple slices and toss to coat.

IN A SKILLET over medium heat, brown the sausage and onion together. Drain well, placing the browned sausage in a sieve and pressing on it with a spoon to drain excess fat.

PUT a layer of the sausage mixture on the bottom crust in the pie pan. Place a layer of coated apples on top of it, then the remainder of the sausage, and finish with a final layer of apples.

ROLL out the top crust until it is large enough to cover the pie with at least 1 inch of overhang and place over the filling. Brush the top with beaten egg yolk. Cut a few slits in the top crust. You can take the leftover scraps of dough and cut hearts, leaves, or other shapes to place on top of the pie. The crust with the egg yolk brushed on becomes a deep golden brown, while the unbrushed cutouts remain lighter, letting them stand out better. Trim the edges of the crust so that they overhang the pastry dish by about 1 inch. Pinch the edges of the top and bottom crusts together to seal, then fold them under and tuck them into the pastry dish. Flute the edges with your fingers or a fork.

BAKE the pie for 30 minutes, and then reduce the oven temperature to 350°F and bake for another 30 minutes. Serve these lovely little browned pies warm.

NOTE: *To save time, you can use premade crusts found in the refrigerator section of your grocery store.*

the crooked road

Virginia's Heritage Music Trail is a 250-mile route that winds through the scenic terrain of the region. Although the trail is focused on the uniqueness and vitality of this region's music heritage, it also includes outdoor recreational activities, museums, crafts, and historic and cultural programs.

In Hiltons, Scott County, you'll find the "Carter Family Fold." This Carter Family Music Center preserves old-time country and folk music with a performance stage, a museum, and the original log cabin where A. P. Carter grew up. On any given weekend in years past, visitors were often surprised by the appearance of June Carter and Johnny Cash performing on the stage.

In Galax, attend the "Old Fiddler's Convention," which has been going on for almost one hundred years. A visit to Bristol will find you at the original home of country music and the "Birthplace of Country Music Alliance." In August, 1927, downtown Bristol hosted two weeks of recording sessions for the Victor Recording Company. The music recorded in those two weeks influenced generations of country, bluegrass, gospel, and rock and roll musicians. In Bristol, Victor talent scout Ralph Peer discovered Jimmie Rodgers, the Carter Family, and Ernest "Pop" Stoneman. These recordings, now known as the "Bristol Sessions," have been heralded by scholars as "the big bang of country music," and by musicians like Johnny Cash as "the most important event in the history of country music." These sessions can still be heard at the Alliance.

Event after event and sight after glorious sight takes place along the Crooked Road. Steeped in history and nature, the road is well worth traveling.

GARLIC-CHEESE GRITS SOUFFLÉ

serves 6

THE 4½ STREET INN in Highlands, North Carolina, is nestled in the cool elevations of the Blue Ridge Mountains. There's nothing like waking up to clean mountain air and the chirping of birds to remind you of how gentle life can be. You won't want to get out of bed, but if you don't, you might miss out on this wonderfully delicious soufflé. It's simple to make, and that touch of garlic sets it apart.

1 cup quick-cooking grits

8 ounces Velveeta cheese, cut into ½- to 1-inch cubes

8 tablespoons (1 stick) unsalted butter, cut into ½-inch slices

1 clove garlic, minced

3 egg whites

PREHEAT the oven to 325°F and grease or spray a medium soufflé or casserole dish.

COOK the grits according to the package directions. Remove from the heat and add the cheese, butter, and garlic, stirring until the cheese and butter have melted. Cover and let sit until cool.

WHIP the egg whites until stiff, and then fold them into the cheese grits. Transfer the mixture to the prepared casserole dish. Bake for 30 to 40 minutes. Serve immediately.

GOOD MORNING GRANOLA

makes 8 cups

THIS RECIPE FROM FOX MANOR in Kingsport, Tennessee, was a winner in the annual baking contest during Jonesborough Days in 2006. Kingsport, which was once called Christianville, is rich in history. Bays Mountain is a range that extends from the Long Island on the Holston River in Kingsport to Blount County, Tennessee, some 115 miles to the southwest. The Cherokee referred to the easternmost part of the mountain as "Sentinel Point" and jealously guarded possession of the river. The first Europeans recorded seeing the mountain in 1673. Because the river met the Great Warrior's Path, years of contention ensued. It was also the starting point of Daniel Boone's Wilderness Road. Long Island was the jumping-off point for the settlement of central Tennessee and Kentucky. Just before Christmas in 1779, a flotilla of flatboats left Long Island on the long and hazardous voyage down the Tennessee and up the Cumberland to establish Cumberland Colony, the first permanent white settlement in middle Tennessee.

This Fox Manor recipe is a great breakfast before your own wilderness trek. It can be stored in an airtight container for up to 1 month. It also freezes well.

---

5 cups old-fashioned rolled oats

1 cup coarsely chopped walnuts or pecans (Fox Manor uses walnuts)

½ cup firmly packed brown sugar

1½ teaspoons ground cinnamon

½ teaspoon ground nutmeg

1 cup (2 sticks) unsalted butter

⅓ cup maple syrup

½ cup golden raisins

PREHEAT the oven to 350°F. Butter a 10 by 15-inch or larger baking pan.

IN A LARGE BOWL, stir together the oats, nuts, brown sugar, cinnamon, and nutmeg.

IN A SMALL SAUCEPAN over low heat, gently melt the butter with the maple syrup, and then pour the butter mixture over the oat mixture and mix well.

SPREAD into the prepared baking pan and bake for about 30 minutes, or until golden brown, stirring the granola every 10 minutes for even baking. The baking time may vary depending on the size of the pan.

LET the granola cool in the pan. When completely cooled, stir in the raisins and store in an airtight container.

GRITS AND REDEYE GRAVY

serves 6

GRITS DATE BACK FURTHER THAN 1607, when the colonists came ashore at Jamestown, Virginia. They were met by Native Americans offering steaming hot bowls of *rockahominie*, which was softened maize seasoned with salt and animal fat. Some say this classic southern recipe is the only way to eat grits. Others prefer a fancier dish. The fact is that you'll find Redeye Gravy served with almost anything. Folks around these parts love it. Legend has it that Andrew Jackson, a general and the seventh president of the United States, once asked his cook to prepare luncheon. Now, the cook had been drinking corn whiskey the night before, and his eyes were very red. Jackson saw this and asked him to fix country ham and gravy as red as the cook's eyes. Those who overheard this conversation began calling it "redeye gravy," and another southern tradition was born.

---

1 tablespoon ham or bacon drippings

6 slices country ham

½ cup brewed black coffee

6 servings of your favorite grits, prepared according to package directions

IN A LARGE CAST-IRON SKILLET, heat the drippings over medium heat and brown the ham slices on both sides. Add enough water to the skillet to cover the ham, and then cover the skillet and let the ham cook through.

REMOVE the ham from the skillet. Add the coffee to the ham drippings, stirring gently to blend. To serve, place each piece of ham on a plate. Place a mound of grits on the side and cover both with the redeye gravy.

BREAKFAST PIZZA

serves 4

THE FEDERAL GROVE INN in the lovely town of Auburn, Kentucky, is a Federal-style home that was built around 1871 on the site of the first brick home in Logan County, Kentucky. Today, it is one of almost one hundred homes in Auburn listed on the National Register of Historic Places. You'll need 7-inch individual iron skillets to make this breakfast pizza so that everyone gets their own. It's so good that no one will want to share anyway!

1 cup vegetable oil

4 medium potatoes, thinly sliced

8 large eggs

1 cup chopped green onion

1 cup chopped mixed green and red bell peppers

2 cups grated cheddar, Colby, or Monterey Jack cheese

¼ cup mild to medium salsa

HEAT four 7-inch skillets over medium heat and pour ¼ cup of cooking oil into each. Divide the potato slices evenly among the skillets and fry until tender and they start to brown.

BREAK two eggs over the fried potatoes in each skillet, and then add ¼ cup of onion and ¼ cup of bell peppers. Reduce the heat to low, cover the skillets, and let the eggs cook until set.

JUST before serving, sprinkle ½ cup of grated cheese over the egg mixture in each skillet and top with 1 tablespoon of salsa.

SHRIMP AND GRITS

serves 2 to 4

THE INN AT MERRIDUN in Union, South Carolina, is an antebellum mansion listed on the National Register of Historic Places. Situated in the gently rolling upstate region of South Carolina, it is surrounded by shady oaks and century-old magnolias. It was once known as Keenan Plantation, and today the Georgian house is one of the most regal homes in Union. This recipe from the inn combines two southern favorites—shrimp and grits.

---

8 ounces peeled, deveined shrimp

1 tablespoon freshly squeezed lemon juice

Salt and cayenne pepper, or Old Bay seasoning

1 tablespoon olive oil, butter, or bacon grease

½ small yellow onion, finely chopped

¼ cup chopped bell pepper (green, red, or yellow)

¼ cup white wine

2 to 4 cups cooked creamy grits

IN A BOWL, sprinkle the shrimp with the lemon juice and seasonings; set aside.

HEAT the oil in a medium skillet over medium heat and sauté the onion and bell pepper until the onion begins to turn transparent, 7 to 10 minutes. Add the shrimp to the skillet and sauté for about 2 minutes, or until the shrimp turns pink. Transfer to a bowl and set aside.

ADD the wine to the skillet and deglaze the pan, stirring to scrape up any browned bits. Return the shrimp mixture to the skillet and heat just until warm. Serve immediately over the hot grits.

chapter 3

APPETIZERS

BRIE WITH APRICOT

serves 8 to 10

THIS RECIPE IS FROM FOLKESTONE INN in Bryson City, North Carolina. Just a quarter mile from the Great Smoky Mountains National Park and an hour away from charming Asheville, North Carolina, the Folkestone Inn has been entertaining folks for more than seventy-five years. If you visit in March, you can watch the exciting U.S. Whitewater Open at the Nantahala outdoor facility. Recipes for Brie with preserves can be found in other places, many using different ingredients; however, there is something both delicate and slightly tangy about apricots. This is also a very pretty and fresh appetizer.

1 wheel Brie, cut into 8 to 10 equal wedges

3 tablespoons apricot preserves

1 to 2 almond slices per Brie wedge, for garnish

2 to 3 dried apricots, thinly sliced, for garnish

PREHEAT the oven to 400°F.

SLICE each Brie wedge horizontally almost to the outer rind. Dab a small amount of apricot preserves into the sliced middle of each Brie wedge. Dab a drop of preserves on top of each wedge. Place the wedges on a baking sheet and bake for about 5 minutes, or until the middle is soft. Remove from the oven and let cool for 2 minutes. To serve, place each wedge on an individual serving plate and garnish with almond and dried apricot slices.

storytelling

Jonesborough, the oldest incorporated town in Tennessee, is home to the National Storytelling Festival. Each year, writers, local folks, professional storytellers, and outright liars gather to tell tall tales and historic stories. For three days, the first weekend of October, the town is filled with ghost stories, incredible history, and things that are hard to believe.

The ancient art of storytelling is a major pastime in southern Appalachia, and many places have activities centered on the craft. In Bryson City, North Carolina, you'll find the storytelling center of the southern Appalachians and a radio program dedicated to storytelling. There are numerous books on the subject, and luckily, many storytellers and yarn-spinners have been recorded for posterity.

TENNESSEE CHEDDAR PUFFS

makes about 80

STIRRED BY THE MIST that envelops the mountain vistas, the Cherokee people named the Great Smoky Mountains Shaconage, meaning "the place of blue smoke." Before 1900, the area where the Cherokee village stood was called Tuckaleechee Cove, or "peaceful valley," by the Cherokee. In 1900, Wilson B. Townsend and a group of fellow Pennsylvanians formed the Little River Lumber Company; they bought 80,000 acres of land, much of which is now the Great Smoky Mountains National Park. In order to log the rugged terrain and move the logs to the mill, they established the Little River Railroad. The headquarters for both the railroad and the lumber company were located in the village, which was renamed Townsend. At Dancing Bear Lodge, a lovely mountain hotel in Townsend, Tennessee, the Smokies are the back yard. Dancing Bear Lodge's chef was kind enough to share this recipe. Cheese puffs are the perfect appetizer, and these puffs are particularly delightful. Leftover puffs can be frozen and reheated.

---

1 cup (2 sticks) unsalted butter

2 cups water

2 teaspoons sugar

4 teaspoons salt

¼ teaspoon cayenne pepper

2 cups all-purpose flour

8 large eggs

10 ounces grated cheddar cheese

Paprika, for dusting

PREHEAT the oven to 400°F. Line a baking sheet with parchment paper, or use a nonstick baking sheet.

IN A MEDIUM SAUCEPAN over medium heat, melt the butter with the water, sugar, salt, and cayenne. Once the butter is completely melted, add the flour. Reduce the heat to low and stir constantly with a wooden spoon for 1 minute. Pour the mixture into the bowl of a stand mixer and mix with a paddle attachment for 1 minute on medium-low speed to cool the mixture. Increase the speed to medium and add the eggs one at a time, making sure each one is incorporated before adding the next. Fold in the grated cheese.

USE a truffle scoop or two spoons to drop 1-inch balls of batter onto the prepared baking sheet. Dust each puff with paprika. Bake for 10 minutes, and then rotate the pan and bake for 10 more minutes, until golden. Serve warm.

a settler's home

While modern southern Appalachia has kept up with the same building trends as the rest of the country, and in some places you will find old Victorian and Federal houses and in other places charming old farmhouses, in the mountains the log cabin remains the sentimental favorite.

Settlers crafted their homes from the trees on their land. Early Appalachian architecture is a form of folk art that combines the skills of the German, Scotch-Irish, English, and Scandinavian settlers in the southern highlands. At first their cabins were rough, unhewn structures about the length of a good 15- to 30-foot log. To have a window was beyond luxury and very rare. Each cabin had a fireplace, usually made from river rocks, or from clay and sticks, known as *mud and daub*. If a cabin needed to be raised in order to be level, a wooden floor was built. Filling in the spaces between logs is called *chinking*, and the early settlers chinked their homes with mud or a combination of mud and clay.

The entire family lived within the small space, which must have been trying during the winter months as many of the families had six to thirteen children.

The main function of the fireplace, other than keeping folks warm, was to cook the family's food. There would be a table and benches or chairs, small cupboards for storage, trunks for clothing (no closets in those days), and beds. Hanging overhead would be drying vegetables and plants.

Although a cabin dating back to the 1700s would be hard to find now, one can still see second- or third-generation cabins scattered around the area. Many folks keep the cabin on their land when they build a new home. I'm not sure if it's for sentimental

reasons or just because southern Appalachians don't waste anything. I'd like to think that it's sentiment. There was a wedding down the road a few years back and the little old cabin sitting about forty feet from the new log home had been all fixed up and decorated. Someone had put a sign on the door reading "Honeymoon Cabin."

There are living museums all over southern Appalachia where one will find original buildings. The Appalachian Museum in Clinton, Tennessee, is now the home of the Clemens cabin, the home of Mark Twain's parents in Possum Trot, Tennessee. Up in the Smoky Mountain National Park you will find the Farm Museum. It's an incredibly beautiful place where the National Park Service has relocated buildings from farms on former Cherokee land. Be sure to see the cantilevered barn.

IMPERIAL CRAB BALLS

serves about 20

THIS IS A SOUL FOOD RECIPE from the Appalachian region of northern Alabama. My friend J. C. Rivers and I were talking about soul food and why many people outside of the African-American community might find it odd or be afraid to try it. The fact is that most soul food dishes are absolutely delicious. He gave me this recipe and a few others that appear in the book. These little crab balls also taste great when served with a dip, such as a tartar sauce or a cocktail sauce. Enjoy!

Vegetable oil, for deep frying

1 cup crushed unsalted saltine cracker
   (or boxed crumbs)

1 large egg

1 cup mayonnaise

½ teaspoon dry mustard

½ green bell pepper, finely chopped

1 pound fresh or 2 (6½-ounce) cans crabmeat

IN A DEEP FRYING PAN or a deep fryer, heat the vegetable oil to 350°F on a deep-frying thermometer.

PLACE the cracker crumbs in a bowl or on a plate.

IN A SEPARATE LARGE BOWL, combine the egg, mayonnaise, and mustard. Beat well. Add the green pepper and blend well. Stir in the crabmeat. Form ¾- to 1-inch balls and roll them in the cracker crumbs.

DEEP-FRY the balls for 6 minutes, or until golden brown. Drain on paper towels before serving. To serve, place in a chafing dish or other warming dish if you want to serve them heated. They are just as good served simply on a plate.

the black african influence on southern appalachian and american dining

The term soul food appeared in the 1960s. Before that time, these dishes were just good home cookin'. By today's standards, the African diet was far superior nutritionally to the European diet of the settlers. Most Africans lived on greens, vegetables, stews, and melons, while the European diet consisted of heavy breads, fatted meats, butters, and starches. With the plantation culture of the 1700s and 1800s, African foods found their way into the southern Appalachian diet, and southern agriculture soon included African seeds. Foods such as eggplant, sesame seeds, okra, sorghum, sweet potatoes, field peas, peanuts, black-eyed peas, African rice, and melons soon became part of the everyday dinner table.

MUSHROOMS STUFFED WITH RICE AND GREENS

serves 4

THE IRON MOUNTAIN INN BED AND BREAKFAST and cabins is located just above Watauga Lake in the Cherokee National Forest. Set high atop a mountain with a section of the Appalachian Trail along the ridge behind the Inn, they welcome guests from around the world to share the peace and quiet and the glorious views. The Cherokee National Forest is home to about 1,500 black bears, but you probably won't see them. And in the spring that thunderlike roar you hear is the wild mountain turkey finding his mate. If you like to fish, this is the place for you. There are 154 species of fish in the forest. This recipe is from the inn. I can see this as a hot appetizer, two on a plate for luncheon, or as a side to dinner. Try to use mushrooms that are 4½ to 5 inches in diameter. To prevent the mushrooms from becoming waterlogged, remove any sand or dirt with a brush and wipe with damp paper towels instead of rinsing with water.

2 teaspoons extra-virgin olive oil

1 small white onion, chopped

4 cups sliced escarole or Swiss chard

2 large cloves garlic, minced

1 cup brown rice, cooked according to package
  directions

½ cup chopped roasted red bell peppers

4 large portobello mushrooms, stems discarded

½ cup prepared hummus, preferably basil flavored

3 Roma tomatoes, sliced

¼ cup chopped walnuts

¼ cup grated Parmesan cheese

PREHEAT the oven to 400°F.

HEAT the oil in a medium skillet over medium-low heat. Add the onion and cook, stirring occasionally, for 5 minutes, or until softened. Add the escarole and garlic. Cook, stirring occasionally, for 5 minutes, or until wilted. Remove from the heat and stir in the rice and peppers.

PLACE the mushrooms, gill side up, on a rimmed baking sheet. Spread with the hummus and spoon the rice mixture over the top, spreading it to the edges. Arrange the tomato slices on top and sprinkle with the walnuts and Parmesan.

BAKE for 25 to 30 minutes, until the mushrooms are tender. Let stand for 10 minutes before serving.

NOTE: *Although nearly half the calories of hummus come from fat, virtually none of it is saturated. Add olive oil and walnuts and you have a delectable dose of monounsaturated fats to keep you hunger-free for hours.*

CREAM PUFFS WITH CHICKEN SALAD FILLING

makes about 16

BARB LAND, OWNER OF THE SWEETEST TOUCH in Sevierville, Tennessee, is a native southern Appalachian whose family dates back to the early days in the mountains. She's usually busy creating wonderful cakes, pies, breads, and other goodies for her many customers or creating menus for local eateries. However, Barb loves to cook for her friends and neighbors, too. If you're lucky enough to meet her, say hello and order the special. It's sure to be good!

CREAM PUFFS

½ cup water

⅓ cup unsalted butter

⅔ cup all-purpose flour

⅛ teaspoon salt

4 eggs

CHICKEN SALAD

1 (8-ounce) package cream cheese, at room temperature

¼ cup milk

¼ teaspoon salt

⅛ teaspoon dry mustard

⅛ teaspoon freshly ground black pepper

2 tablespoons finely chopped scallions (white and green parts)

½ cup seedless red or green grape halves

⅓ cup chopped walnuts

1½ cups chopped cooked chicken

TO MAKE THE CREAM PUFFS, preheat the oven to 400°F. In a large saucepan, bring the water and butter to a boil. Add the flour and salt. Stir over low heat until the mixture forms a ball. Remove from the heat and add the eggs one at a time, beating well after each addition.

TO FORM THE PUFFS, place 2 tablespoons of batter per puff about 3 inches apart onto an ungreased baking sheet. Bake for 25 minutes, or until puffed and golden brown.

TO MAKE THE CHICKEN SALAD, combine the cream cheese, milk, salt, dry mustard, and pepper in a large bowl. Mix until well blended. Add the scallions, grape halves, walnuts, and cooked chicken and stir until well blended.

LOWER the oven to 375°F. Cut the tops off of the puffs. Fill each puff with chicken salad and replace the top. Put the filled puffs on a baking sheet and bake for 5 minutes, or until warmed. Serve immediately.

BLUE CHEESE BALL

serves 12 to 15

THIS RECIPE FROM THE CLAY CORNER INN in Blacksburg, Virginia, is a classic. The inn is located next to Virginia Tech, and visiting parents and many a football fan have enjoyed this tasty cheese ball while gathering there in the evening.

---

2 teaspoons Worcestershire sauce

¼ cup chopped fresh parsley

8 ounces blue cheese, crumbled

2 (8-ounce) packages cream cheese, at room
   temperature

1 cup finely chopped walnuts

Toasted bread rounds or crackers, for serving

IN A MEDIUM BOWL, combine the Worcestershire sauce and parsley. Blend well. Add the blue cheese and mix well. Add the cream cheese and blend until smooth. Cover and refrigerate the mixture until firm, about 2 hours. Form the mixture into a large ball and roll the ball in the chopped nuts. Serve with toasted bread rounds or crackers.

the appalachian trail

More than 2,175 miles long, this footpath meanders through the Appalachian Mountains and fourteen states from Georgia to Maine. The scenic trail was conceived by Benton MacKaye, a Massachusetts regional planner and forester for the U.S. Forest Service. He wanted the trail to provide leisure, enjoyment, and the study of nature for people living in the urban areas of the eastern United States. The trail was completed in 1937. Whether you are on a short hike, a day trip, or a long backpacking journey, the trail is an excellent way to view the wild scenery, woodlands, animals, wildflowers, and magnificent vistas that are the

Appalachian Mountains. Watched over by the National Park Service and the Appalachian Trail Conservancy, this incredible trek is enjoyed by millions of visitors each year.

WARM CAMEMBERT SALAD WITH APPLES AND WALNUTS

serves 6

TERRELL HOUSE BED AND BREAKFAST sits on a quiet street near historic downtown Burnsville, North Carolina. Burnsville, with its quaint shops and coffeehouses surrounding a public square, has been called the "Gateway to the Blue Ridge." and is a true mountain community, with cool summer breezes, clean air, and an easy pace. The Mt. Mitchell Crafts Fair has been going on for more than fifty-three years and is just one of the fun things to experience in Yancey County. This Camembert salad is a little appetizer the inn serves before a dinner party, and their guests seem to like it a lot. It would also make a good side or luncheon salad.

---

1 (8-ounce) wheel Camembert cheese

7 ounces lamb's lettuce or baby spinach

2 sweet apples, peeled, cored, and cut into
    bite-size pieces

2 tablespoons chopped walnuts, toasted (see Note)

½ cup white wine vinaigrette, homemade
    or store-bought

PREHEAT the oven to 400°F.

PLACE the pastry shells on a baking sheet and bake for 10 minutes, or until golden brown. Remove the shell tops (if your pastry shells have them), and reserve for garnish or another use.

REMOVE the rind from the Camembert and cut the cheese into 6 wedges. Place a wedge into each partially baked shell. Bake for 15 minutes, or until the cheese is bubbly and brown on top.

WHILE the pastry shells are baking, combine the lettuce, apples, walnuts, and vinaigrette in a large bowl and toss well. Place each pastry shell on an individual serving plate and add the shell top, if desired. Distribute the salad evenly around each shell and serve.

NOTE: *To toast chopped walnuts, shell the walnuts, remove any loose skin, and chop them. Preheat the oven to 350°F and lightly spray or grease a baking pan (or use a nonstick pan). Spread the walnuts in a single layer and bake for 5 to 7 minutes, until the nuts become golden brown and fragrant.*

MISSISSIPPI SIN

makes 4 cups

THERE ARE VARIATIONS OF THIS RECIPE out there using soup mixes, but this version uses only fresh ingredients and is the best I've ever tried. Serve it with the bread you cut out of the middle of the loaf to make the bread bowl, but have some toasted rounds or other crackers on hand in case you use up all of the bread. This is one appetizer that won't last long. You might want to double the recipe if you're serving more than eight people.

---

1 (1-pound) round French bread loaf

1 (8-ounce) package cream cheese, at room
    temperature

2 cups grated cheddar cheese

1½ cups sour cream

½ cup chopped cooked ham

⅓ cup chopped sweet onion

⅓ cup chopped green or red bell pepper

⅛ teaspoon Worcestershire sauce

PREHEAT the oven to 350°F.

CUT a thin slice off the top of the bread. Cut a very thin slice off the bottom so that it will sit flat on your serving platter. Then, cut out the middle of the bread to form a bowl for the dip, being careful not to cut through the crust. Reserve the bread that you cut out of the middle.

TO MAKE THE DIP, combine the cream cheese, cheddar cheese, sour cream, ham, onion, bell pepper, and Worcestershire sauce in a large bowl. Mix well until smooth.

FILL the bread bowl with the dip, put the bread top back on, and wrap the whole thing in aluminum foil. Bake for 1 hour. Remove the foil and take the top off the bread loaf. Place in the middle of a pretty dish or platter, tear the reserved bread from the center into pieces suitable for dipping, and arrange them around the bread bowl. Serve immediately.

ONION-CHEESE DIP

makes 6 cups

THIS EASY AND DELICIOUS DIP is from the Blue Mountain Mist Country Inn in Sevierville, Tennessee. The inn is one of those places where you can sit on the large porch and look out over acres of green grass to the mountains. Once when visiting friends from Europe who were staying there, I found them out on the lawn in their bare feet, reading about the Great Smoky Mountains and just enjoying the peace and clear mountain air. Make sure you use Hellmann's mayonnaise for this dip because it will not separate. Hellmann's is sold all over the United States, though it sometimes goes by the name Best Foods. You can make this recipe two ways. If you bake it uncovered, you'll get a hot and bubbling browned dip. If you cover your baking dish, it won't brown. This recipe is good served with crackers, toasted rounds, or vegetables.

2 cups chopped sweet onions

2 cups grated Swiss cheese

2 cups Hellmann's or Best Foods mayonnaise

PREHEAT the oven to 350°F. In a large bowl, combine the onions, cheese, and mayonnaise and mix well. Pour into a small baking dish or covered casserole dish and bake for about 25 minutes, or until bubbling. Serve hot.

Education

"I HAVE LEARNED THAT SUCCESS IS TO BE MEASURED NOT SO MUCH BY THE POSITION THAT ONE HAS REACHED IN LIFE AS BY THE OBSTACLES WHICH HE HAS OVERCOME WHILE TRYING TO SUCCEED. OUT OF THE HARD AND UNUSUAL STRUGGLE THROUGH WHICH HE IS COMPELLED TO PASS, HE GETS A STRENGTH, A CONFIDENCE, THAT ONE MISSES WHOSE PATHWAY IS COMPARATIVELY SMOOTH BY REASON OF BIRTH AND RACE."

—Booker T. Washington

From the beginning, the pioneers in southern Appalachia made education a priority. Literary societies flourished, and books were treasured. When readers could not go to a library, librarians brought books to them on packhorses.

The isolated and rural nature of the region meant that education came in the form of the one-room schoolhouse. Churches sent front men to evaluate the need for schools. Based on reports that furthered the Appalachian myth of poverty, social deprivation, and moral decay, missionaries soon followed. These early educators believed that self-help through labor and crafts production would change the Appalachian family and bring them out of "squalor." This elitist view was insulting, as few Appalachian people lived in squalor and it only built up the myth of the poor Appalachian.

The Presbyterian Church brought the log cabin college system to East Tennessee. Other denominations soon followed, and by 1850 there were at least twelve denominational colleges in the region. After the Civil War, many churches sent missionaries to the southern Appalachians to work with freed slaves, and later with the mountain whites. By 1900 there were more than 200 mission schools in southern Appalachia. Many were settlement schools. In addition to traditional studies, these schools offered medical assistance, health education, nutrition, and hygiene, vocational and agricultural training, recreational services, and social welfare. The schools were self-sufficient communities. Children who lived close by lived at the school all week. In some cases, children were even sent to schools in nearby states.

In 1869, Lincoln Memorial University was built in the Cumberland Gap. In 1864, Laura Scott Cansler received permission from Union Army General Ambrose Burnside to open a school for free blacks during the occupation of Knoxville. In 1914, after years of accomplishment in education and as a lawyer, her son, Charles Warner Cansler, introduced adult night school classes for working people.

Former slave Booker T. Washington became director of the Tuskegee Institute in 1881. In 1896, George Washington Carver became head of the agricultural department. His work improved southern agriculture immeasurably. Far from the myth, southern Appalachian education has thrived for generations and continues to do so today.

HOT ARTICHOKE DIP

makes about 6 cups

THIS RECIPE IS FROM THE COLLINS HOUSE INN, a completely renovated early 1920s colonial-style home in the heart of historic downtown Marion, Virginia. In the 1600s the area around Marion was Native American land, but in 1745 a land grant opened the area to settlement. I've been told that there are visitors to the inn who will take the pie plate and eat the whole thing, so this recipe is often doubled.

1 (8-ounce) package cream cheese, at room
   temperature
1 cup mayonnaise
⅓ cup finely chopped white or yellow onion
1 (14-ounce) can artichoke hearts, drained and chopped
1 tablespoon finely minced garlic
½ cup grated Parmesan cheese
Potato chips or crisp crackers, for serving

PREHEAT the oven to 375°F. In a large bowl, combine the cream cheese and mayonnaise and blend until smooth. Add the onion, artichoke hearts, and garlic, and blend. Stir in the Parmesan. Pour into a 9-inch glass pie plate and bake for 15 to 18 minutes, until golden and bubbling. Serve warm with potato chips or crackers.

SIMPLE SEAFOOD DIP

makes about 1½ cups

THIS DIPPING SAUCE IS SO SIMPLE that you'll want to use it over and over again. To spice it up a bit, use a Cajun cocktail sauce. This goes well with all kinds of cooked cold shellfish, such as crab or shrimp.

1 (8-ounce) package cream cheese,
   at room temperature
½ cup cocktail sauce

IN A SMALL BOWL, beat the softened cream cheese until creamy. Slowly add the cocktail sauce, blending well. Cover with plastic wrap and refrigerate until ready to serve. Beat once more before serving.

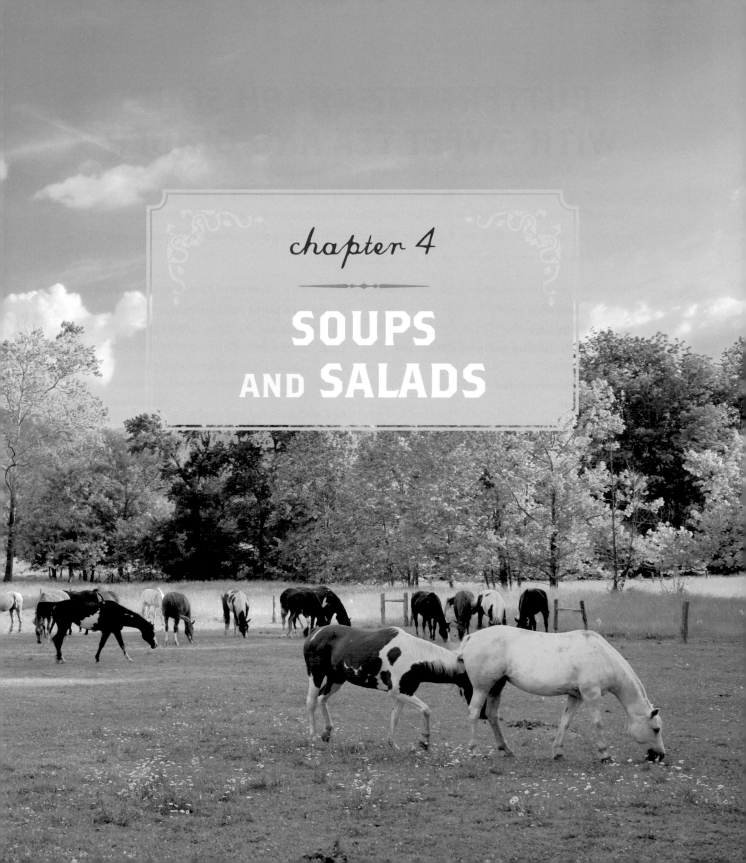

chapter 4

SOUPS
AND SALADS

PEPPER POT SOUP

serves 8 to 10

THIS OLD RECIPE FROM THE CHEROKEE is delicious. This is the kind of soup that you can add your favorite vegetables to, depending on whatever is available. It's good in any season. I like to use red bell peppers, crookneck squash, and pattypan squash along with the other ingredients. However, the original recipe is wonderful just as it is.

---

1 pound beef short ribs

2 large white or yellow onions, quartered

3 ripe tomatoes, peeled and chopped

1 large red, orange, or yellow bell pepper, seeded and diced

1 large turnip, peeled and cubed

½ cup diced potato

½ cup sliced carrots

½ cup corn kernels (drained canned or defrosted frozen)

¼ cup minced celery

Salt and freshly ground black pepper

PUT the ribs in a large pot and pour water over them until the water covers the meat by about 1 inch. Cover and bring to a boil over high heat, and then reduce the heat and simmer for 2½ hours, or until the meat is done.

REMOVE the meat and let it cool, reserving the liquid in the pot. Discard the beef bones and return the meat to the pot. Add the onions, tomatoes, bell pepper, turnip, potato, carrots, corn, and celery. Cover and simmer for 1 to 1½ hours, or until the vegetables are tender.

SEASON to taste with salt and black pepper. Serve immediately.

VEGETABLE CREAM SOUP

serves 6 to 8

THERE IS A FAMOUS DINNER SHOW in Pigeon Forge, Tennessee, that serves the best creamy vegetable soup. It's light and incredibly delicious. Folks come away from that show scheming and plotting, determined to discover the secret of the well-guarded recipe. This isn't it, but it's as close as it comes. Because the original soup is so fresh tasting, I have listed only fresh ingredients here. Use a food processor or blender to puree the vegetables. It will take a little longer to make, but it's worth it.

---

4 cups chicken broth

½ cup pureed fresh peas

½ cup pureed fresh whole-kernel sweet corn

½ cup chopped and pureed fresh green beans

½ cup chopped and pureed fresh carrots

1 small clove garlic, peeled and pureed

1 small sweet onion, chopped and pureed

1 scallion, chopped and pureed

Vegetable salt (I use Vege-Sal)

2 cups half-and-half

IN A LARGE POT, bring the chicken broth to a low boil. Add the vegetables, one at a time, stirring after each addition. Lower the heat to medium and cook for about 5 minutes. Add vegetable salt to taste. Cook for a few more minutes to blend the flavors, stirring occasionally.

TURN the heat down to a simmer. Slowly add the half-and-half, stirring constantly until well blended. Cook for another 2 to 5 minutes, stirring constantly, and serve immediately.

CHICKEN-CABBAGE SOUP

serves 6

THIS IS A GREAT SOUL FOOD RECIPE. There is nothing as satisfying as a good chicken soup. Folks in the mountains eat a lot of cabbage, and the addition of cabbage to this classic soup makes it even heartier—and I think more delicious. I like to use skin-on chicken and remove the skin from the chicken after cooking. It makes a tastier broth. For a truly lean broth, remove the skin before cooking and then strain the broth through cheesecloth.

5 cups water

2 boneless chicken breasts

2 chicken bouillon cubes, crushed

3 cups finely shredded green cabbage

2 large tomatoes, peeled and chopped

1 cup shredded carrots

1 large sweet onion, finely chopped

½ cup thinly sliced celery

½ teaspoon salt

1 teaspoon freshly ground black pepper

IN A LARGE POT over medium-low heat, combine the water, chicken breasts, and bouillon cubes. Cover and cook until the chicken is cooked through, about 1 hour. Test the meat for doneness by cutting through it with a knife. If necessary, cook for an additional 30 minutes.

REMOVE the chicken from the pot and set aside to cool. Strain the broth to remove any large particles, and return the broth to the pot. Reduce the heat to low.

ADD the cabbage, tomatoes, carrots, onion, and celery to the broth. Cook for about 30 minutes, or until the vegetables are tender, stirring occasionally.

WHILE the vegetables are cooking, remove the skin and bones from the chicken breasts and chop the meat into small cubes. Discard the skin.

TASTE the broth and season with the salt and black pepper. Stir.

WHEN the vegetables are cooked through, add the chopped chicken. Stir and cook for an additional 10 to 15 minutes. Taste the soup and adjust the seasonings before serving hot.

CREAM OF PEAR SOUP

serves 10

BUILT AT THE TURN OF THE CENTURY as part of the legal Mountain Rose Distillery Number 250, the Mountain Rose Inn in Woolwine, Virginia, is nestled along the banks of Rock Castle Creek and within the shadows of the Blue Ridge Mountains. The inn shared this original recipe with me. It's a wonderful luncheon treat or first course for a warm summer day. Sweet homemade bread or muffins on the side add just the right touch.

---

7 ripe, juicy pears

⅓ cup sugar

½ teaspoon ground nutmeg

1 (12-ounce) can frozen white grape–peach juice concentrate

1 (8-ounce) carton French Vanilla Cool Whip

Fresh mint leaves, for garnish

PEEL, halve, and core the pears. Arrange the halves on a single layer in a microwave-safe baking dish and sprinkle them with the sugar and nutmeg. Add enough water to cover the bottom of the dish. Microwave the pears until tender, 4 to 6 minutes. Set aside to cool.

PLACE the frozen juice concentrate and the Cool Whip in a blender and blend until smooth. Add the pears and blend until the mixture forms a souplike consistency.

CHILL the soup in the refrigerator and garnish with mint leaves just before serving.

COLD SWEET POTATO SOUP

serves 6

THIS RECIPE IS A NICE TWIST on the traditional vichyssoise. Native to the Americas, sweet potatoes are very common in the mountains and throughout the South. One can find sweet potato as the main ingredient in almost every cooking category. George Washington Carver can be thanked for the popularity of this wonderful-tasting vegetable. It was the Tuskegee Institute, where he did his research, that promoted the crop to aid farmers in the southern region who were having difficulties. This soup can also be served warm. Don't be surprised if this becomes one of your favorites.

4 large sweet potatoes, quartered

2 tablespoons unsalted butter or margarine

1 medium sweet onion, chopped

1 cup shredded carrots

½ cup finely chopped celery

2½ cups chicken broth

Pinch of ground nutmeg

Salt

¼ cup half-and-half

PLACE the sweet potatoes in a large saucepan and cover them with water. Bring to a boil and cook until the potatoes are tender. Drain the water, remove the skins from the sweet potatoes, and set the potatoes aside.

PLACE the butter, onion, carrots, and celery in the saucepan over medium heat. Sauté until tender and the onions are clear. Add the broth, nutmeg, and sweet potatoes. Bring to a boil, and then reduce the heat to a simmer. Cover and cook for 40 minutes. Taste and add salt if needed. Let the soup cool, and then puree it in a blender or food processor. Slowly pour in the half-and-half and process just until smooth. Chill in the refrigerator before serving.

WILD GREENS SALAD

serves 2 to 4

BACK IN THE DAY, the southern highlanders gathered from the wild, and many still do. One friend is known to gather from any spot she finds a plant. Her son will say, "Now, Mother, you just cain't go on folks' land and take they's wild things." To which she replies in a gruff voice, "Awuk!" I see her now and then by my place "transplanting" what she wants for her garden. I asked her how she got the wild plants to grow and she told me the secret: "You plant them in the direction they was growing when you found them." Although this is a greens salad, you can add tomatoes, carrots, peas, or any other favorite vegetable.

SALAD

1 cup finely chopped wild onions, shallots, or sweet onions

4 cups watercress

1½ cups loosely packed dandelion leaves

¼ cup firmly packed sheep sorrel

MAPLE DRESSING

⅓ cup sunflower oil

⅓ cup cider vinegar

3 tablespoons maple syrup

¾ teaspoon salt

¼ teaspoon freshly ground black pepper

TEAR the greens into bite-size pieces and place them in a salad bowl. Toss to combine, and refrigerate while you make the dressing.

TO MAKE THE DRESSING, pour the oil, vinegar, and maple syrup into a large jar with a lid. Add the salt and pepper, put the lid on the jar, and shake vigorously. Set aside to let the flavors blend for about 20 minutes.

TO SERVE, shake the dressing again and pour the desired amount onto the greens. Lightly toss to coat all of the greens.

greens

Southern mountain folk have traditionally used everything available to them for food, and wild greens are no exception. Greens to a southerner are mostly kale, collard, turnip, spinach, and mustard greens. And serving enough greens for a family dinner is referred to as "making a mess o' greens."

Collard greens are vegetables akin to the cabbage family. Old superstitions say that collards served with black-eyed peas and a hog jowl on New Year's Day bring a year of good luck. Hanging a fresh collard leaf over your door will scare off evil spirits, and a fresh leaf placed on the forehead will cure a headache.

FREEZER COLESLAW
makes 3 pints

CLAY CORNER INN IS NEXT TO the Virginia Tech campus in downtown Blacksburg. It's got all the amenities of a fine hotel and the friendly atmosphere of a small inn. The owner was kind enough to share this recipe with me. It was her grandmother's recipe, and I like it because it's prepared ahead of time and then thawed when you're ready to use it. This slaw will keep for up to a year in the freezer.

---

1 medium head green cabbage, shredded
(about 5 cups)
1 teaspoon salt
1½ cups sugar
1 cup vinegar
½ cup water
1 teaspoon celery seed
4 medium stalks celery, chopped (about 2 cups)
1 small green bell pepper, chopped (about ½ cup)
1 medium carrot, cut lengthwise in thin, short slices
(about ½ cup)
1 small onion, chopped (about ¼ cup)

IN A LARGE BOWL, mix the cabbage and salt and let it stand for at least 1 hour.

IN A SAUCEPAN over medium heat, bring the sugar, vinegar, water, and celery seed to a boil. Boil and stir for 1 minute, and then remove the pan from the heat and let the mixture cool to lukewarm.

DRAIN the cabbage, return it to the bowl, and stir in the celery, green pepper, carrot, and onion. Add the vinegar mixture to the cabbage mixture and stir to combine. Spoon the slaw into three 1-pint freezer containers and freeze until ready to use.

ABOUT 8 hours before serving, transfer a container of slaw to the refrigerator to thaw. Drain well before serving.

BROCCOLI SALAD, SOUTHERN-STYLE

serves 4

THIS IS A SOUL FOOD RECIPE for a pretty salad that makes a colorful presentation at a luncheon or dinner table. The addition of seedless raisins gives it just a touch of sweetness, and the shredded cabbage and sweet onions give it that southern "down home cookin'" touch.

SALAD

4 cups broccoli florets

2 cups shredded red cabbage

1 medium sweet onion, finely chopped

1 cup seedless raisins

1 tablespoon finely chopped fresh parsley

2 large carrots, shredded

CELERY SEED DRESSING

1½ cups mayonnaise

⅓ cup sugar

¼ cup cider vinegar

½ teaspoon seasoned salt

¼ teaspoon freshly ground black pepper

¼ teaspoon celery seed

IN A SERVING BOWL, combine the broccoli, cabbage, onion, raisins, parsley, and carrots. Toss to blend, and then cover the mixture and refrigerate it for 1 hour.

WHILE the salad is chilling, make the dressing. In a large jar with a lid, combine the mayonnaise, sugar, vinegar, seasoned salt, pepper, and celery seed. Put the lid on the jar and shake well. Let rest in the refrigerator for 1 hour.

TO serve the salad, pour the chilled dressing over the chilled salad and toss to completely coat the vegetables. Cover the salad once again and chill in the refrigerator for 20 minutes to 1 hour, or until ready to serve.

CORN RELISH SALAD

serves about 8

THIS IS A WONDERFUL PICNIC SALAD. The first time I ate corn relish salad was at a company picnic. My boss proudly made it, and I couldn't stop eating it! I can't tell you who won the three-legged race, but I'll never forget this salad. Fresh corn is best, but you can use canned.

———— ◆ ————

3 cups cooked fresh corn kernels cut off the cob

⅓ cup sugar

2 medium tomatoes, finely chopped

¼ cup chopped sweet onion

½ cup chopped green bell pepper

½ cup chopped red bell pepper

½ teaspoon celery seed

¼ teaspoon salt

¼ cup vegetable oil

⅓ cup vinegar

1 cup shredded Colby cheese

IN A LARGE BOWL, combine all of the ingredients and stir gently. Cover and refrigerate for 4 hours or overnight. Stir well before serving.

southern appalachian quilting

By the seventeenth century, quilted clothing was fashionable in England and France. Fine quilting was a sign of wealth, but the poor quilted as well. If they couldn't afford wool or cotton, old blankets, clothing, or even feathers, straw, or leaves were used. In English orphanages and poorhouses, one kind of bedcovering was made by sewing paper into cotton bags.

Immigrants brought quilting to America, and Appalachian women have quilted ever since. They had only the clothing they came with, and so quilts were pieced together using old fabrics. If you wanted to sleep under a cover, you had to make a quilt. Women saved scraps of fabric and created wonderful patterns. The American patchwork quilt seems to have begun from this. A bit of a wedding dress, a baby's bib, or a husband's shirt gave the quilt a special touch, and the quilt was usually passed down through generations, often telling a family's story. There are quilt shops all over the southern mountains with wonderful fabrics and patterns, and if you're a "fabric-aholic" like I am, the temptation is overwhelming.

WARM POTATO SALAD

serves 8

THIS RECIPE IS FROM THE PROSPECT HILL INN in Mountain City, Tennessee. Mountain City is located in the Blue Ridge Mountains on the Daniel Boone Heritage Trail and is the county seat of Johnson County, and it's surrounded by magnificent peaks and spectacular fishing and mountain sports. This recipe is a nice change from the usual cold salad served at picnics and family gatherings. This is one of those recipes that spans the seasons, but it's especially yummy on a chilly day.

1½ pounds medium boiling potatoes

½ cup vegetable oil

3 tablespoons all-purpose flour

½ cup mild-flavored vinegar, such as rice vinegar

1½ cups water

2 tablespoons sugar

1¼ teaspoons salt

Freshly ground black pepper

1 egg yolk, slightly beaten

1 medium onion, diced

1 cup sliced celery

COOK the potatoes in boiling salted water until just done. Peel the potatoes while they're warm, and then slice them ⅓ inch thick. You should have about 4 cups of potato slices.

MEANWHILE, blend the oil with the flour in a large saucepan over medium heat. Gradually add the vinegar and water, stirring until smooth and thick. Stir in the sugar, salt, and pepper. Stir about 1 tablespoon of the hot mixture into the beaten egg to temper it, and then pour the egg mixture into the saucepan and cook, stirring constantly, for 6 to 8 minutes, until the egg is cooked thoroughly.

ADD the warm potatoes, onion, and celery and mix well. Serve warm.

CABBAGE SALAD

serves 8

ROCKWOOD MANOR IN DUBLIN, Virginia, is located along Virginia's Crooked Road Heritage Trail. It's a 130-year-old architectural gem nestled among 68 secluded acres in the heart of the New River Valley. Frances Bell, who built the house, was an adept cattle trader. In his travels he met and married Sarah James Kent in 1855. During the "Great Unpleasantness" it is believed that the Bells furnished cattle, horses, and crops to the Confederacy.

SALAD

2½ to 3 cups shredded green cabbage (about ½ head)

1 cup shelled sunflower seeds

1 bunch scallions, finely chopped

8 ounces slivered almonds

2 packages beef ramen noodles (reserve the flavor packets)

RAMEN DRESSING

½ cup sugar or Splenda

¾ cup vegetable oil

⅓ cup white vinegar

Reserved flavor packets from the ramen packages

PREHEAT the oven to 350°F. Lightly grease a baking sheet and set aside.

IN A LARGE BOWL, combine the cabbage, sunflower seeds, and scallions.

PLACE the slivered almonds onto the prepared baking sheet. Toast them in the oven for 7 to 10 minutes, until they become golden brown and fragrant. Watch them carefully and do not let them burn. Place them on a wire rack to cool completely.

ADD the cooled almonds to the cabbage mixture. Crumble the ramen noodles into the cabbage mixture. Mix well.

TO MAKE THE DRESSING, place the sugar, oil, vinegar, and beef flavor packets in a jar with a lid. Put the lid on the jar and shake it vigorously.

JUST BEFORE SERVING, add the dressing to the cabbage mixture and toss well to coat.

chapter 5

VEGETABLES
AND BEANS

VEGETABLE PIE

serves 8

A GOOD VEGETABLE PIE can be served anytime and anywhere. In the winter, it can be a hearty breakfast. It's also a nice brunch or luncheon dish. At the dinner table it's a great way to serve vegetables. This pie is fun to make because you can experiment with your favorite vegetables. If you don't care for zucchini or mushrooms, substitute your favorite squash or peas. If you aren't fond of black pepper, you might want to lower the amount used.

---

3 tablespoons unsalted butter

2 medium zucchini, thinly sliced

2 medium, fat, yellow crookneck squash, thinly sliced

1 large sweet onion, finely chopped

¾ cup southern seasoned collard greens, drained (see Note), or fresh chopped spinach 1½ cups whole small white mushrooms, sliced, or 3 (4-ounce) cans (pieces and stems)

2 red bell peppers, seeded and chopped

1 medium tomato, diced

½ teaspoon garlic powder

1 tablespoon chopped fresh thyme

2 small Roma tomatoes, thinly sliced

6 large eggs

½ cup half-and-half

½ teaspoon vegetable salt (such as Vege-Sal)

1½ teaspoons freshly ground black pepper

2 cups packed grated Monterey Jack or Colby cheese

1 (8-ounce) package cream cheese, at room temperature

1 (9-inch) unbaked piecrust (page 147)

PREHEAT the oven to 350°F.

MELT the butter in a large heavy pot over medium heat. Add the zucchini, squash, onion, greens, onion, mushrooms, bell peppers, diced tomato, garlic, and thyme. Sauté for 15 minutes, or until the vegetables are just tender. Add the sliced tomato and stir gently. Remove the pan from the heat and set it aside to cool while you prepare the egg mixture.

WHISK the eggs, half-and-half, vegetable salt, and black pepper together in a large bowl. Stir in the cheese and cream cheese. Gently mix in the vegetables, and then pour the mixture into the pie crust.

BAKE for about 1 hour, or until the egg mixture begins to brown on top and bubble at the edges. Let stand for 10 minutes, and then cut into wedges and serve warm.

NOTE: *I use the Margaret Holmes brand of seasoned collard greens because they are delicious and go well with eggs.*

BEANS BILLABONG

serves 8

THE CLAIBORNE HOUSE BED AND BREAKFAST INN is an 1895 Queen Anne Victorian surrounded by beautiful English-style gardens. It's an elegant and unique historic home in Rocky Mount, Virginia, on Virginia's Crooked Road Heritage Music Trail in the Blue Ridge Mountains. There's something to do almost every night in Franklin County. Folks gather to hear mountain musicians play and join in on the fun. In one place five dollars will pay the band and get you dinner. In another you'll have to bring your own chair. Most places have free admission, but donations are gladly accepted. I like this recipe because it's a slightly different way to serve green beans. The owner calls it Beans Billabong after her birthplace, Australia, and the guests seem to really enjoy it.

---

6 slices bacon

2 cloves garlic, minced

5 cups fresh green beans, trimmed, or 4 (8-ounce) cans green beans

¼ cup grated Parmesan cheese

Freshly ground black pepper

HEAT a large skillet over medium heat. Cook the bacon until crispy, and then transfer it to paper towels to drain and cool. Once it's cool, crumble it and set aside.

REMOVE some of the bacon grease from the skillet, but leave a generous coating on the inside of the pan. Add the garlic and sauté until it begins to brown slightly. Stir in the green beans and heat for 5 to 8 minutes, until the green beans start to lose their bright color. Toss in the Parmesan and season with black pepper. Add the crumbled bacon to the mixture. Toss everything together and serve hot.

leather breeches

Southern Appalachians can thank the Cherokee for "leather breeches." The Cherokees taught early mountain people this wonderful way to save and store green beans, and it's still a useful way to make your garden last through the winter.

After you've picked some green beans, string them on a piece of string and hang them in the sun or a warm dry place by the fire. Let them dry completely.

In the early days you would have seen leather breeches hanging from a rafter close to the fireplace where the cooking was done. The modern way is to put the dried beans in plastic bags, string and all, and store them in the freezer. It will keep insects from sharing them.

To fix a mess of beans, take some beans off the string and soak them in water for 2 hours. Pour off the water and put the beans in a large pot on the stove. Add fresh water, bacon, and salt to taste. Cook until done.

BOURBON–SWEET POTATO CASSEROLE

serves 6 to 8

THIS RECIPE FROM THE 1869 SHAKER TAVERN BED & BREAKFAST in South Union, Kentucky, is yummy! South Union was established in 1807 by the Society of Believers, or Shakers. At its zenith, the village covered 6,000 acres and had 350 members. The community closed in 1922, leaving hundreds of buildings, some of which are still standing, including the central living quarters. Today, the remaining buildings make up the Shaker Museum at South Union, and the tavern operates as visitor lodging.

CASSEROLE

3 cups mashed cooked sweet potatoes

1 cup granulated sugar

8 tablespoons (1 stick) unsalted butter, melted

2 large eggs

1 teaspoon vanilla extract

⅓ cup milk

1 teaspoon Maker's Mark or your favorite bourbon

TOPPING

½ cup firmly packed brown sugar

¼ cup all-purpose flour

½ cup chopped pecans

4 tablespoons (½ stick) unsalted butter, at room
   temperature

PREHEAT the oven to 350°F.

USING a stand mixer on medium speed, beat the sweet potatoes, granulated sugar, butter, eggs, vanilla, milk, and bourbon for about 5 minutes, or until smooth and creamy. Pour the mixture into a 2-quart baking dish.

TO MAKE THE TOPPING, combine the brown sugar, flour, and pecans in a medium bowl. Mix well. Add the butter and mix. Evenly sprinkle the topping over the top of the potatoes.

BAKE the casserole for about 20 minutes, or until it bubbles. Serve hot.

GRILLED OKRA
WITH PINE NUTS
serves 4

THE CREEKWALK INN at Whisperwood Farm in Cosby, Tennessee, has an "on the ranch" feeling in the Great Smoky Mountains. In the first half of the twentieth century, Cosby was known by east Tennesseans as the "Moonshine Capital of the World." Like other southern Appalachian communities, Cosby's main crop was corn, and during rough times they put that to advantage. These days Cosby is a quiet community and Creekwalk Inn is a delightful place to visit. Don't be surprised if you see an elk walk by the window! With the subtle elegance of toasted pine nuts and the down-home goodness of okra, this recipe works just as well for a cookout as it does for a gourmet dinner.

1 tablespoon olive oil

½ cup pine nuts

1 pound okra, washed and patted dry
   (do not trim stems)

Zest of 1 lemon

HEAT the olive oil on a griddle or in a small skillet over medium heat. Add the pine nuts and toast them until they begin to turn golden brown, stirring or tossing often. Transfer the toasted pine nuts to a dish or plate to cool.

PUT the okra pods on the griddle or in the skillet and cook for about 12 minutes, turning as needed until seared on all sides.

TO SERVE, sprinkle the pine nuts and lemon zest over the okra.

SAUSAGE-STUFFED MUSHROOMS

makes about 20

THE MAISON BELIVEAU BED AND BREAKFAST in Blacksburg, Virginia, sits on 165 acres of rolling land bordered by forest and spring-fed ponds within the New River Valley and Roanoke Valley. You can go white-water rafting, shop for antiques, visit museums, enjoy a day of wine tasting at local wineries, or, in April, visit the annual International Street Fair and Parade. These stuffed mushrooms are a good accompaniment to a glass of wine. The recipe yield depends on the size of the mushrooms used. Keep in mind that the mushrooms shrink a bit when cooking. Medium-size mushrooms will make delicious little nibbles on your appetizer table. I also like to use large stuffed mushrooms as a side to a meat dish.

20 large white mushrooms

8 ounces bulk sausage (turkey sausage for a milder taste)

1 (8-ounce) package cream cheese, at room temperature

PREHEAT the oven to 350°F. Lightly butter a 9 by 13-inch baking dish and set aside.

WASH the mushrooms and remove and reserve the stems. Finely chop the reserved stems and set aside. In a large skillet over medium heat, brown the sausage; drain to remove excess fat. Reduce the heat to a simmer and add the cream cheese. Stir to blend. Add the chopped mushroom stems and stir. Let the mushrooms continue to simmer for about 5 more minutes, or until stems are softened.

STUFF the mushroom caps with a heaping amount of the sausage mixture. Place in the prepared baking dish and bake for 30 minutes. Serve warm.

RAMPS AND BACON

serves 4

RAMPS (*ALLIUM TRICOCCUM*) ARE AN ONION, or scallion, or leek-type vegetable that grow wild in the area roughly between North Carolina, New England, and Minnesota. The harvest season is from late March to early May. Ramps are an acquired taste and some say they're "stinky," but they make many tasty dishes. You can serve them simply with bacon, as in this recipe, or in soups, salads, and other dishes.

---

2 pounds ramps, cleaned and trimmed

8 ounces sliced bacon

½ cup water

Salt and freshly ground black pepper

CUT the ramp bulbs from the leaves and set both aside.

IN A LARGE SKILLET over medium heat, cook the bacon until crispy. Transfer to paper towels to drain and cool.

POUR off all but 2 tablespoons of the pan drippings. Add the water and the ramp bulbs to the skillet. Cook over medium heat, stirring occasionally, for 15 minutes, or until the bulbs are soft. Coarsely chop the ramp leaves and add them to the pan. Cook them until they wilt.

CRUMBLE the bacon and add it to the pan. Cook until all the liquid has been absorbed. Season with salt and black pepper and serve hot.

ramps

The name *ramp* is believed to have come from the British Isles, where a similar wild plant, ramson, grows. The early English settlers in the 1500s, recognizing the similarity, named the native plant, and the name has been shortened to *ramps*. Early mountain people used to hunt for ramps in what is now the Great Smoky Mountains National Park. When the park was formed, that became illegal, but enough wild ramps were "transplanted" by mountain folk that availability isn't a problem.

The ramp has long been valued by the residents of southern Appalachia for its medicinal properties. The Cherokee and mountain settlers made "spring tonics" from ramps, and children with "ramp odor" are said to have been asked to stay out of school for a few days. Ramp festivals have sprung up all over the area. While Richwood, West Virginia, calls itself the "Ramp Capitol of the World," I'm not sure they can compete with the annual Cosby, Tennessee, Ramp Festival. The festival has had some famous attendees, including President Harry Truman; Tennessee Ernie Ford, who was from Bristol, Tennessee; Eddie Arnold; Roy Acuff; Bill Monroe; Dorothy Collins; Minnie Pearl; Brenda Lee; and Dinah Shore.

APPALACHIAN CIDER BEANS

serves 8

THE FIRST TIME THAT I TASTED CIDER BEANS was at the local gas station. Here, in the mountains, folks gather at the local gas station to visit, have a meal, and catch up on the local news. Far from serving "fast food," these little places present "home cookin'" and it's delicious. This good ol' mountain recipe is very satisfying paired with cornbread or muffins.

———◆———

3 cups dried pinto beans

3 cups fresh apple cider

8 ounces salt pork, thinly sliced

2 small yellow onions

6 tablespoons sorghum molasses

1 tablespoon dry mustard

2 teaspoons salt

PICK over the beans and discard any stones and wrinkled beans. Rinse well and place in a large bowl. Add cold water to cover by 3 inches, cover, and let soak for 12 hours.

DRAIN the beans and transfer them to a heavy saucepan. Add the cider and bring the beans slowly to a boil over medium heat. Boil gently, uncovered, for about 30 minutes. Remove from the heat and drain the beans, reserving the cooking liquid.

PREHEAT the oven to 300°F.

LAYER half of the salt pork slices on the bottom of a 2-quart ceramic bean pot or other deep baking dish. Spoon the beans into the bean pot, and then bury the onions in the beans.

IN A SMALL SAUCEPAN, combine the sorghum molasses, dry mustard, and salt and place over medium heat to dissolve the mustard and salt. Pour the hot mixture evenly over the beans, and top with the remaining salt pork slices. Pour in the reserved cooking liquid and add hot water as needed to cover the beans. Cover the bean pot.

BAKE for 4 hours, and then uncover the pot and add more water if the beans seem too dry. Re-cover and continue to bake for 1 to 2 hours, until the beans are tender. Serve hot directly from the pot.

EASY CHILI 'N' HOPS

serves 8 to 10

CHILI IS A FAVORITE throughout the southern states, and in the mountains it's no different. Every year there is a chili cook-off in one place or another. This recipe from the Sweetest Touch in Sevierville, Tennessee, has a unique flavor. I went down to the gas station one day to get a cold root beer when I saw Barb Land, owner of the Sweetest Touch, and her daughter eating a bowl of chili. After saying my "howdy's" I said, "Well, that looks good." Barb answered, "Go get you some." So I went behind the counter and ladled out a bowlful. I'd never had chili with beer in it before and I thought it tasted quite good, although I prefer dark beer that has molasses as an ingredient.

---

1 (4-ounce) can whole roasted chilies

1 pound ground chuck or lean hamburger

1 large sweet onion, diced

¼ teaspoon paprika

¼ teaspoon ground cumin

¼ teaspoon cayenne pepper

1 teaspoon dried oregano

¼ teaspoon garlic powder

2 (15-ounce) cans meatless chili beans

2 (15-ounce) cans kidney beans, rinsed and drained

3 large tomatoes, cored, chopped, and mashed
   (reserve the juice)

2 medium tomatoes, diced

1 cup tomato juice

1 (12-ounce) can beer (not light beer)

PLACE a colander in the sink and turn on the cold water. Open the can of chilies and dump them into the colander. Let the water run over them while you put paper towels on a plate. With the water running, use your fingers to slit them open and remove the seeds and middle vein. (Be sure to get all of the seeds—they're hot! And do not remove any burned parts on the skin.) Lay the cleaned chilies on the paper towels to drain. (Wash your hands well to remove any oils from the chilies, which can irritate your skin.)

IN A LARGE HEAVY SKILLET over medium heat, cook the ground chuck until browned. Drain off the juices. Chop the drained chilies and add them to the skillet. Stir to blend. Mix in the onion, paprika, cumin, cayenne, oregano, and garlic powder and sauté, stirring occasionally, for about 8 minutes.

TRANSFER the contents of the skillet to a kettle or large saucepan. Let simmer over low heat. Add the chili beans and kidney beans and stir to blend. Stir in the mashed tomatoes and their reserved juice, the diced tomatoes, and the tomato juice. Blend and allow the mixture to heat up, and then add the beer. Stir to blend.

COVER the kettle and simmer for 1 hour before serving.

RED BEANS AND RICE

serves 4

THIS IS A VERY TRADITIONAL SOUL FOOD RECIPE that can be found throughout Appalachia and other parts of the South. The farther south you go, the spicier it gets. I like to use spicy turkey sausage because it's easier on the stomach than plain sausage and better for you. Serve this with cornbread and greens and you have a hearty meal.

4 cups dried red kidney beans

2 large raw ham hocks

4 cloves garlic, chopped

1 tablespoon bacon drippings

3¼ cups water

1 medium yellow onion, chopped

1 green bell pepper, seeded and chopped

8 ounces bulk spicy sausage, cooked and drained

Pinch of salt

Pinch of freshly ground black pepper

Pinch of cayenne pepper (optional)

1½ cups white rice, cooked according to package directions

PICK over the beans and discard any stones and wrinkled beans. Rinse well and place in a large bowl. Add cold water to cover by 3 inches, cover, and let soak for 2 hours.

DRAIN the beans and transfer them to a large pot. Add the ham hocks, garlic, and bacon drippings. Cover with the water. Bring the mixture to a boil over medium heat. Reduce the heat to a simmer and cook for 1 hour and 30 minutes, or until the meat on the hocks loosens from the bone. Stir in the onion, bell pepper, and sausage. Add the salt, black pepper, and cayenne pepper. Bring to a boil over medium heat, and then reduce the heat to low and simmer for 1 hour.

LET rest for 15 to 20 minutes, and then serve over the rice.

chapter 6

BREADS,
MUFFINS, ROLLS,
and BISCUITS

KHACHAPURI (GEORGIAN CHEESE BREAD)
makes two 7-inch round loaves

THIS IS A MELUNGEON RECIPE, though it didn't start out that way. Tracing a recipe's history can be fascinating. The Caucasian War, between the Caucasia region and the Russian Empire, lasted from 1817 to 1864. Between 1834 and 1897 almost half a million people immigrated to the United States from the Caucasus. According to genealogical records, some of them ended up in southern states. I don't know if this recipe came from them or how it ended up in the Melungeon community. What I do know is that you are going to love this cheese bread. Serve it with a bowl of fruit as a delicious breakfast, or as a side to luncheon or dinner.

2 cups all-purpose flour

3 tablespoons vegetable oil

¾ cup plain yogurt

1 tablespoon cornstarch

¾ teaspoon baking soda

¼ teaspoon salt

½ cup crumbled feta cheese, or ¼ cup crumbled Roquefort cheese

1 cup grated mozzarella cheese (or Georgian suluguni cheese)

1 large egg, beaten

1 teaspoon unsalted butter

IN A MEDIUM BOWL with a wooden spoon, beat ⅓ cup of the flour with the oil. Add the yogurt and mix well. Stir in ⅓ cup more flour. Sift the cornstarch, baking soda, and salt together, and stir them into the flour mixture. Gradually stir in enough of the remaining flour to make a soft but not sticky dough. Lightly dust the dough with more flour, cover with a kitchen towel, and let rest at room temperature for 1 hour. With a wet fist, punch it down. Cover and let it rest for another hour, and then punch it down again.

MEANWHILE, soak the feta in water to cover for 10 minutes, then drain it. In a medium bowl, mix the feta or Roquefort, mozzarella, and egg. Shape the cheese mixture into two medium balls and set aside.

DIVIDE the dough into two portions and roll each into a ball. On a floured surface, flatten each ball into a 7-inch round. With floured hands, gently rotate the dough and pull and stretch the rounds into two 10-inch circles about ¼ inch thick. Be careful not to tear the dough. Pat each cheese ball into a 5-inch circle and place each one on the center of a dough circle. Gently pull up the edges of each piece of dough, plcating and pinching it to enclose the cheese. Pat each into a 7-inch round.

HEAT a large cast-iron or nonstick skillet over low heat for 3 minutes. Melt a little of the butter in the skillet, just to film it lightly. Place one loaf of bread seam side up into the skillet. Cover and cook for 12 minutes over very low heat, shaking the pan occasionally. Uncover the skillet and flip the bread over. Re-cover and cook over low heat for about 12 minutes, or until the bread is deep golden brown. Remove the bread from the skillet, lightly brush the top with butter, and let it stand for 5 minutes. Repeat with the second loaf.

USE a serrated knife to cut the bread, and serve it warm.

arts and crafts

Sometime around 1937, the Great Smoky Mountains arts and crafts community began. Known as "the Glades," it's located just outside of Gatlinburg, Tennessee, high in the mountains. The original artists would walk into Gatlinburg, sell their wares to the few tourists at the time, and walk back home to the Glades. Wood carver John Cowden and a few friends wanted to be near their tools and families, so they decided to stay at home and invite the tourists to come to them. As the tourists started coming, other artists joined them, and what is now an eight-mile stretch of hands-on studios was created. There are more than 200 artists and craftspeople working in little studios, small malls, and private homes along the way. People are welcome to sit and watch the artists work or just have a friendly chat. This mountain area has been designated as a Tennessee Historic Arts Trail.

Arts and crafts communities are not only found in Gatlinburg, but also throughout the southern mountains. The Southern Highland Craft Guild, in Asheville, North Carolina, offers galleries, a library, education, and a crafts fair. The Appalachian Arts and Crafts Center in Clinton, Tennessee, is a nonprofit organization whose mission is to promote Appalachian artists through education and sales. A visit to the Qualla Boundary (page 5) will introduce you to Cherokee arts and crafts. Northern Georgia is home to some formidable crafts organizations, and along Virginia's Crooked Road, arts and crafts are featured in little shops, in museum workshops, and at fairs. Appalachian arts and crafts range from homemade candles, dolls, brooms, and soap to folk art to more sophisticated forms, and all are truly treasures from southern mountain culture.

JOHN CRIPE'S FRY BREAD

makes 1 large or 2 small rounds

THIS IS A NATIVE AMERICAN RECIPE and is a staple for feasts, powwows, special dinners, and cultural gatherings. John Cripe is a descendant of the Eastern Band of the Cherokee nation, whose members lived and still live in the Great Smoky Mountains. While walking on the Trail of Tears, his ancestors managed to escape and set their own path to freedom. Fry bread can be found, in one version or another, in almost every culture of the world. Most fry bread is made from white flour, but John's addition of wheat flour makes this bread really tasty. After the rounds cool a bit, you can dust then with a cinnamon-sugar mixture or confectioners' sugar, or spread them with Tennessee Honey Cream (recipe follows). We've had some good conversations over this round bread with a hole in the middle.

1¼ cups whole wheat flour

1¼ cups all-purpose flour

1 tablespoon baking powder

1 teaspoon salt

½ cup sugar (optional)

¼ cup vegetable oil, plus more for frying

2 large eggs

1 cup water

MIX the whole wheat flour, all-purpose flour, baking powder, salt, and sugar in a large bowl.

MAKE a well in the center of the dry ingredients and add the vegetable oil, eggs, and water. Stir just until the dough feels like it will be easy to work with in your hands.

LIGHTLY coat your hands with oil and dust them with flour. Knead the dough with your hands until it is elastic. If necessary, add just enough all-purpose flour to keep the dough from sticking to your hands.

WHEN the dough is ready, tear off a piece about the size of a tennis ball and set it on a floured towel or board. Flour your hands and shape it into a circle about 10 inches in diameter and ¼ inch thick. Make a hole in the center about 1½ inches in diameter. Repeat with the remaining dough.

HEAT a heavy skillet or deep fryer with enough vegetable oil so that the dough will be able to float, about 2 cups. The hot oil should be about 350°F on an instant-read thermometer. Don't let it get hot enough to smoke.

CAREFULLY add the dough round or rounds to the hot oil with a spatula, being careful to not splash hot oil on yourself. Fry the bread for about 5 minutes on each side, or until golden brown. You may have to fry the bread in batches. Remove the bread from the oil and drain on paper towels. Repeat with the remaining dough rounds as necessary. Let cool a bit, and serve warm.

Tennessee Honey Cream

makes 2 cups

Tennessee Honey Cream is one of my favorite sweet toppings for breads, including fry bread. Make it the day you plan to use it, since the whipped cream will begin to separate if you leave it in the refrigerator for more than a day.

2 cups heavy cream
2 teaspoons honey (preferably mountain honey)

IN A MEDIUM BOWL using a stand mixer, beat the cream on medium speed until it begins to thicken. Drizzle in the honey and continue to beat until the whipped cream is thick.

MELUNGEON FRIENDSHIP STARTER AND BREAD

THIS RECIPE IS A TRADITIONAL MELUNGEON BREAD with a purpose. Not only is this a very good bread, but a little extra starter was also always made to pass on to friends and neighbors. It's the gift that keeps on giving. To keep the starter going, include the recipe when you pass on a batch.

Starter
makes about 4 cups

1 cup sugar
1 cup all-purpose flour
1 cup milk

USE a wooden or plastic spoon to combine the sugar, flour, and milk in a large glass bowl. Cover the bowl loosely with cheesecloth and secure the cloth to the bowl with rubber bands. Store at room temperature for 17 days, stirring the starter once every day. Do not stir on the 18th, 19th, 20th, or 21st day.

ON THE 22ND DAY, remove the cheesecloth and stir in the following:

1 cup sugar
1 cup all-purpose flour
1 cup milk

THAT DAY, give 1 cup of starter each to 2 friends and keep the remaining 2 cups for yourself. To keep the starter going, do not refrigerate the remaining starter.

Bread

makes two 9-inch loaves

1 cup starter (page 88)

⅔ cup vegetable oil

3 large eggs

½ teaspoon vanilla extract

1 cup sugar

2 cups all-purpose flour

½ to 1 teaspoon ground cinnamon

½ teaspoon salt

1½ teaspoons baking powder

1 cup dark raisins

1 cup chocolate chips

1 cup chopped nuts

1 cup chopped apples or dried dates (optional but a tasty addition)

PREHEAT the oven to 350°F. Grease and lightly dust with sugar two 5 by 9 by 3-inch loaf pans.

IN A LARGE BOWL, combine the starter, oil, eggs, vanilla, and sugar and mix well. In a medium bowl, whisk together the flour, cinnamon, salt, and baking powder. Stir the flour mixture into the starter mixture until just combined. Fold in the raisins, chocolate chips, nuts, and apples.

POUR the batter into the prepared loaf pans and bake for 45 minutes, or until a skewer or table knife inserted into the center of the loaves comes out clean. Let cool on a wire rack. Wrap any leftover bread and refrigerate. It will keep for about a week.

synchronized fireflies

Synchronized lightning bugs are the subject of much study and entertainment. These delightful creatures can be found only on the Asian continent and inside the Great Smoky Mountains National Park, at Elkmont. They live at an elevation of 2,200 feet, and when taken from their natural surroundings, they cease being synchronous! It is a scientific mystery.

Every year in June, people from all over the world gather to watch as the lightening bugs perform their wonderful dance in the forest. As the forest darkens, thousands of fireflies light up and blink six times, stop for about three seconds, and then start again. This show goes on for some time and is absolutely beautifully amazing to watch.

Outside of the park, nonsynchronized fireflies are a magical addition to spring nights in the mountains. The profusion of dancing lights appears at dusk and is so beautiful and mezmerizing to watch that hours can pass by without you even realizing it.

IRISH SODA BREAD

makes one 9-inch round loaf

WHEN YOU ARRIVE AT FOX MANOR in Kingsport, Tennessee, you are likely to notice the original carriage steps used by passengers to disembark in the days of horse-drawn carriages. This is your first clue that you're at a unique and historic inn. Built in the late 1800s, Fox Manor is one of Kingsport's oldest homes. This recipe for Irish soda bread won the Annual Baking Contest at Jonesborough Days in 2006.

4½ cups all-purpose flour

5 teaspoons baking powder

1½ teaspoons salt

1 teaspoon baking soda

1 cup (2 sticks) butter

2 large eggs

1 cup sugar

1 cup milk

1 cup buttermilk

1 tablespoon caraway seed

¾ cup golden raisins, soaked in warm water for 30 minutes and drained

¾ cup dark raisins, soaked in warm water for 30 minutes and drained

PREHEAT the oven to 325°F. Grease a 9 by 4-inch round cake or springform pan. You can also use a deep angel food or tube pan.

IN A LARGE BOWL, sift together the flour, baking powder, salt, and baking soda. In a separate large bowl, cream together the butter, eggs, and sugar until light and fluffy.

COMBINE the milk with the buttermilk in a small bowl. Fold the flour mixture into the butter mixture alternately with the milk mixture. Stir in the caraway seeds and the raisins.

SPOON the batter into the prepared pan. Bake the bread for about 1½ hours, or until a skewer or table knife inserted in the center comes out clean. Let cool on a wire rack.

ORANGE-CRANBERRY SCONES

makes about 2 dozen

BUILT AROUND 1890, Sunrise Farm Bed and Breakfast sits on ten acres in the Blue Ridge Mountain foothills of northwest South Carolina. The farm is the last part of an early 1900s 385-acre cotton plantation. The area is a haven for fishermen, boaters, hikers, birdwatchers, and nature lovers. I have always loved scones. The first time I ate them was in a Victorian tearoom, and I found them delicious. They were plain scones, and I remember thinking that they would be good with this or that ingredient added. The flavors of orange and cranberry blend so well that this recipe is going to become a favorite from your kitchen. Serve them with butter and a cup of hot cranberry tea. In the summer a tall glass of Southern Sweet Tea (page 174) is a lovely complement.

---

2 cups all-purpose flour

¼ cup sugar

1 tablespoon baking powder

½ teaspoon baking soda

½ teaspoon fine sea salt

¾ cup cold unsalted butter, cut into pieces

1½ tablespoons grated orange zest

1 cup dried cranberries, soaked in boiling water for
    5 minutes, drained, and patted dry

1 cup cold heavy cream or half-and-half, or more
    if needed

1 teaspoon vanilla extract (optional)

Cinnamon sugar, for topping

PREHEAT the oven to 400°F. Line a baking sheet with parchment paper.

IN A BLENDER or food processor, combine the flour, sugar, baking powder, baking soda, and salt. Using the pulse setting, cut in the cold butter until the mixture resembles coarse meal.

TRANSFER the mixture to a large cold bowl and mix in the orange zest and cranberries. Add the cream and vanilla, mixing until the dry ingredients are moistened. This may take more than 1 cup of cream; if so, gradually add more cream 2 tablespoons at a time until the dough holds together.

SHAPE the dough into a ball and place it on a lightly floured surface. Use a rolling pin to roll the dough to a ½-inch thickness. Cut into 2-inch rounds with a biscuit cutter.

PLACE the scones close together, but not touching, on the prepared baking sheet. Brush the tops with cream and sprinkle with cinnamon-sugar mixture. Bake for 12 to 15 minutes, until golden brown.

BUTTERMILK-BLACKBERRY SCONES

makes 8

MIRACLE FARM BED AND BREAKFAST SPA RESORT is a certified organic inn located on twenty-five acres in Floyd, Virginia, along Virginia's Crooked Road Historic Music Trail. It shares its land with Miracle Farm, a nonprofit animal sanctuary. Since blackberries grow wild all over the mountains, I'm always happy to find another blackberry recipe, and this one is lovely. It's one of those versatile, add-your-favorite-ingredient recipes that are fun to make. You might want to use blueberries, raspberries, or strawberries instead of the blackberries. Any ingredient that tastes good with orange will work nicely.

⅔ stick unsalted butter, melted

1 teaspoon grated orange zest

1 tablespoon Grand Marnier

1¾ cups whole wheat pastry flour

1 teaspoon baking powder

½ teaspoon baking soda

⅔ cup sugar

⅓ cup golden raisins

⅔ cup buttermilk

1 cup fresh blackberries (or other berries, fresh or frozen)

PREHEAT the oven to 400°F. Lightly grease a baking sheet.

IN A SMALL BOWL, combine the melted butter, orange zest, and Grand Marnier. Let it sit as you mix the other ingredients.

IN A LARGE BOWL, mix the flour, baking powder, baking soda, and sugar together. Add the raisins and stir to coat them.

STIR the buttermilk into the melted butter mixture, then mix it in with the dry ingredients. Gently fold in the blackberries. Shape the dough into a ball and place it on a lightly floured surface. Divide the dough into eight equal-size mounds and place them on the baking sheet. Bake for about 20 minutes, or until golden brown. Let cool on a wire rack.

OATMEAL-BLUEBERRY MUFFINS
makes 1 dozen

BERRY SPRINGS LODGE IS A RELAXING Great Smoky Mountains bed-and-breakfast resort retreat in Sevierville, Tennessee. You can see breathtaking views from the porches, which overlook a mist-covered valley and the higher mountains. You can stroll along the trails or fish the nearby Little Pigeon River, explore the area, and return to a delicious dinner. This recipe is not only healthy, but also very good. Serve them with Blueberry Butter (recipe follows).

———◆◆———

8 tablespoons (1 stick) unsalted butter, melted

½ cup sugar or Splenda

2 egg whites or 2 large eggs

¾ cup crushed pineapple, well drained

¾ cup all-purpose flour

2¼ teaspoons baking powder

1 teaspoon ground cinnamon

1 cup quick-cooking oats

1 cup fresh blueberries or dried cranberries

PREHEAT the oven to 350°F. Line a standard muffin pan with liners.

IN A MEDIUM BOWL, combine the butter and sugar and blend until creamy. Mix in the egg whites (or whole eggs) and the drained pineapple.

IN ANOTHER MEDIUM BOWL, sift together the flour, baking powder, and cinnamon. Add the flour mixture to the butter mixture and blend well. Mix in the oats, and then fold in the blueberries.

FILL the muffin liners to the tops with the batter. Bake for 20 to 25 minutes, until a toothpick inserted into the centers of a couple of muffins comes out clean. Let cool on a wire rack. Wrap and keep in the refrigerator.

Blueberry Butter
makes 1¾ cups

1 stick unsalted butter, at room temperature

1 cup fresh blueberries

¼ cup confectioners' sugar

IN A MEDIUM BOWL, combine the butter, blueberries, and confectioners' sugar and blend well. Pack the mixture into a butter mold or place it in a serving container and chill it in the refrigerator before using.

I LOVE BACON MUFFINS

makes 1 dozen

IMAGINE THESE MUFFINS SERVED with scrambled eggs or an omelet for breakfast. They would also be good served with a luncheon salad or Wild Greens Salad (page 63). This down-home muffin is a real treat served with Sweet Onion Butter (recipe follows), and you just may have to make more of both.

2 cups sifted all-purpose flour

1 tablespoon baking powder

¼ teaspoon salt

1 tablespoon sugar

1 tablespoon bacon drippings

1 cup milk

2 large eggs, well beaten

6 slices bacon, cooked until crisp, drained, and crumbled

PREHEAT the oven to 400°F. Lightly grease a standard 12-cup muffin pan and place it in the oven to heat.

IN A LARGE BOWL, sift together the flour, baking powder, salt, and sugar. Add the bacon drippings, milk, and eggs and stir to blend. Fold the crumbled bacon into the batter and mix until blended. Spoon the batter into the hot muffin pan.

BAKE for 15 to 20 minutes, until golden brown. Let cool on a wire rack.

Sweet Onion Butter

makes ¾ cup

8 tablespoons (1 stick) unsalted butter, at room temperature

¼ cup finely grated sweet onion

½ teaspoon garlic powder

IN A MEDIUM BOWL, combine the butter, onion, and garlic powder and blend well. Pack the mixture into a butter mold or place it in a serving container and chill it in the refrigerator before using.

NOTE: *The butter will keep for about 4 days in the refrigerator. It can also be heated and served as a sauce over steak, hamburgers, or vegetables.*

WHIPPED CREAM BISCUITS

makes about 1½ dozen

SUCH A SIMPLE RECIPE, these Melungeon biscuits are light and creamy. Serve them with Strawberry Butter (recipe follows) for a special treat. Biscuits are a staple at the southern Appalachian table. Restaurants serve biscuits covered in lots of melted butter as an appetizer. Breakfast comes with biscuits covered in sausage gravy. Lunch and dinner often come with biscuits, gravy optional. A large biscuit covered in gravy is even considered a meal. There is nothing quite as delicious as a fresh homemade biscuit and this recipe is delicious. Enjoy these biscuits with flavored butter or with Chocolate Gravy, a southern Appalachian classic.

1 cup heavy whipping cream

2 cups all-purpose flour

1 tablespoon baking powder

¾ teaspoon salt

PREHEAT the oven to 350°F. Lightly grease a baking sheet.

BEAT the whipping cream with a stand mixer on medium speed until it forms stiff peaks. Sift together the flour, baking powder, and salt and gently fold it into the whipped cream until it forms a soft dough.

TURN the dough out onto a floured surface and roll it out to a thickness of ½ inch. Using a floured biscuit cutter, cut out biscuits and place them on the prepared baking sheet. Bake for 15 minutes, or until golden brown. Let cool on a wire rack and serve warm.

Strawberry Butter

makes about 2 cups

1 cup (2 sticks) unsalted butter, at room temperature

3 tablespoons confectioners' sugar

¾ cup fresh strawberries, hulled

PLACE the butter in a blender, add the confectioners' sugar and strawberries, and blend until smooth. Pack the mixture into a butter mold or place it in a serving container and chill it in the refrigerator before using.

Chocolate Gravy

serves 4 to 6

This is a Melungeon recipe and an Appalachian tradition. Mexican chocolate could have been traded from Spanish Louisiana into the Tennessee Valley and introduced as breakfast chocolate to the Appalachians. Or the Melungeons already living in the southern Appalachian Mountains could have brought chocolate gravy with them from the Spanish colonies. No one is completely sure. This may seem strange to many folks, but the tradition of eating chocolate with breads goes back to Europe. I had a French teacher in school (bless her heart, I gave her such a hard time) who told us that children in France are given bread with chocolate tucked inside as a treat; and the Spanish make a kind of pastry covered in chocolate for breakfast. This recipe has been handed down from generation to generation. It's delicious on homemade biscuits or served over buttered toast with bacon on the side.

2 cups water

1 tablespoon unsalted butter

3 tablespoons unsweetened cocoa powder

½ cup all-purpose flour

½ cup sugar

¼ teaspoon salt

2 cups milk

PUT the water in a medium saucepan over medium heat and bring it to a boil. Add the butter, turn the heat to low, and cook until the butter is completely melted.

IN A SMALL BOWL, mix together the cocoa, flour, sugar and salt. Add enough milk to make a paste, stirring to blend. Pour the remaining milk into the saucepan. Let the mixture in the saucepan come to a boil again, and then slowly pour the paste mixture into the water mixture. Stir constantly until it thickens into a gravy. Serve hot.

WHEAT GERM BISCUITS
makes 12 to 14

BUILT IN 1860, Tanasi Hill Bed and Breakfast is a four-acre wooded estate with lovely period furnishings in historic Greeneville, Tennessee. Greeneville sits in the foothills of the Appalachian Mountains. The Nolichucky River, a major stream draining the Blue Ridge Mountains, is close by, and also nearby is the University of Tennessee in Knoxville. Greeneville is Tennessee's second oldest town and was founded in 1783. Before Tennessee was Tennessee, it was known as the State of Franklin, and Greeneville was its capitol. It is the home and burial place of Andrew Johnson, the seventeenth president of the United States, and Davy Crockett was born in nearby Limestone. This is the innkeeper's mother's biscuit recipe. They are great served hot with the Honey Butter that follows or with assorted jellies.

---

2 cups all-purpose flour

¼ cup wheat germ

1 tablespoon baking powder

½ teaspoon salt

⅓ cup vegetable or canola oil

⅔ cup milk

PREHEAT the oven to 400°F.

IN A MEDIUM BOWL, combine the flour, wheat germ, baking powder, and salt. Blend well. Slowly stir in the oil and milk until it forms a dough. Turn out the dough onto waxed paper. If the dough is sticky, add a little flour and knead it until it is not sticky anymore.

DO NOT roll out the dough; just pat it down until it is about 1 inch thick. Using a biscuit cutter or a drinking glass, cut out rounds and place them on a baking sheet. Bake for 10 to 15 minutes, until lightly browned. Let cool on a wire rack.

Honey Butter
makes ¾ cup

8 tablespoons (1 stick) unsalted butter, at room
    temperature

¼ cup honey

½ teaspoon finely shredded lemon zest

IN A SMALL BOWL, combine the butter, honey, and lemon zest and blend well. Pack the mixture into a butter mold or place it in a serving container and chill it in the refrigerator before using.

YAM CAKES (OR YAM BISCUITS)

makes 1 to 1½ dozen

THIS IS A TRADITIONAL CHEROKEE RECIPE. The Cherokee gathered wild sweet potatoes, or yams, and also cultivated their own vines. In earlier days they would have baked the yams in the ashes around the fire. These browned orange-colored biscuits are a favorite of mine. They're great with Cinnamon-Maple Butter (recipe follows).

————◆————

2 cups sifted all-purpose flour

2½ teaspoons baking powder

1½ teaspoons sugar

1½ teaspoons salt

½ cup vegetable oil

½ cup milk

1 cup mashed cooked sweet potatoes or yams

PREHEAT the oven to 425°F.

SIFT together the flour, baking powder, sugar, and salt into a bowl. Pour the oil and milk into a measuring cup, but do not stir them.

PLACE the yams in a large bowl, add the oil and milk, and blend well. Add the flour mixture and mix lightly with a fork until the mixture just holds together. Turn out the dough onto a floured surface and knead until smooth, about twelve kneading strokes. Roll the dough out to a thickness of about ¼ inch and cut it into rounds with a floured biscuit cutter or a drinking glass.

PLACE the rounds on an ungreased baking sheet and bake for 10 to 20 minutes, until the yam cakes are golden brown. Let cool briefly on a wire rack, and serve hot.

Cinnamon-Maple Butter

makes about 2 cups

2 cups (4 sticks) butter, at room temperature

2 drops vanilla extract

2 tablespoons pure maple syrup

¼ teaspoon ground cinnamon

IN A MEDIUM BOWL, combine the butter, vanilla, maple syrup, and cinnamon and whip until it is very light (you can use an electric mixer, a blender, a food processor, or a whisk). Pack the mixture into a butter mold or place it in a serving container and chill it in the refrigerator before using.

CORN PONE, TENNESSEE-STYLE

serves 6

CORN PONE, SOMETIMES CALLED INDIAN PONE, is a type of cornbread traditionally made over an open fire in a cast-iron pan. This recipe, however, uses the oven and a baking dish. Beans and cornbread are a staple in the mountains. This dish is good as is, or you may want to add mixed vegetables, tomatoes, or chopped sweet onions to the beans. You can use a lightly greased 9-inch baking dish instead of a cast-iron skillet.

---

2 cups cooked pinto beans (freshly made or canned and drained)

¼ teaspoon freshly ground black pepper

Dash of hot sauce, or 1 tablespoon spicy barbecue sauce (optional)

1 cup cornmeal

1 teaspoon baking soda

½ teaspoon salt

1 large egg, lightly beaten

2 cups buttermilk

2 tablespoons unsalted butter, melted

PLACE an oven rack in the top portion of the oven and preheat the oven to 450°F.

IN A 9- OR 10-INCH oven-safe cast-iron skillet over medium heat, add the beans, pepper, and hot sauce and cook until the beans get very hot. Set aside.

IN A LARGE BOWL, combine the cornmeal, baking soda, and salt and blend well. In a separate bowl, whisk together the egg and buttermilk. Add the butter and whisk to blend. Slowly add the buttermilk mixture to the cornmeal mixture and beat until smooth. Pour the batter over the hot beans.

PLACE the skillet on the top rack of the oven and bake for about 20 to 25 minutes, or until the bread is a rich golden color and the sides of the bread pull away from the sides of the pan. Let cool on a wire rack and serve warm.

SYLVAN FALLS MILL CORNBREAD

makes one 9-inch round

THE HISTORIC SYLVAN FALLS MILL, located in the scenic mountains of northeast Georgia, was built in 1840. It is unique among other gristmills in that it's located below a 100-foot cascading waterfall, and the mill is powered by a 27-foot water wheel, which is one of the largest in the United States. The mill has been renovated and converted into the Sylvan Falls Mill Bed & Breakfast Inn. You can still watch the miller grind fresh flour and grits from the historic water-powered mill. This is their delicious corn bread recipe.

---

4 tablespoons (½ stick) butter

1 large egg

¾ cup milk

¾ cup all-purpose flour

¾ cup stone-ground cornmeal

1 tablespoon baking powder

1 tablespoon sugar

1 teaspoon coarse salt

MELT the butter over low heat in a 10-inch heavy skillet with a lid.

IN A MEDIUM BOWL, beat the egg and then add the milk. Pour in the excess butter from the skillet (about 3 tablespoons).

MIX the flour, cornmeal, baking powder, sugar, and salt together and then add them to the wet ingredients, stirring to mix them well.

POUR the batter into the buttered skillet and cover the skillet. Cook on the stovetop over low heat for 15 to 20 minutes, until the cornbread is set on top and golden brown on the bottom. You may need to turn the pan occasionally to make sure the bottom cooks evenly and does not get too browned in any one spot.

SERVE the corn bread directly from skillet, or turn it out onto a warm plate to serve.

HUSHPUPPIES

makes 2 dozen

THERE ARE A FEW STORIES about how this recipe got its name. One version says that a group of nuns went to New Orleans from France in 1727 and created *croquettes de maise* from the local cornmeal. Another version says that an African cook in Atlanta, Georgia, was cooking up some catfish and croquettes when a puppy began to bark. She put a plate of croquettes before the dog and said, "Hush, puppy!" Southerners love to tell stories, so the truth may never be known. What is true is that hushpuppies are so favored that you will find them as a side at some of the best restaurants throughout the region. In the mountains, hushpuppies are an old favorite.

Vegetable or corn oil, for deep frying

2 cups fine stone-ground white cornmeal

1 tablespoon sugar

2 teaspoons baking soda

2 teaspoons salt

1 tablespoon minced onion

1 large egg

1 cup buttermilk

5 tablespoons cold water, as needed

HEAT the oil in a deep fryer to 360°F.

IN A LARGE BOWL, sift together the cornmeal, sugar, baking soda, and salt. In a small bowl, combine the onion, egg, and buttermilk and beat until frothy. Pour the buttermilk mixture into the cornmeal mixture and stir lightly to mix. Add just enough of the cold water to make a good dropping dough.

DROP the dough by tablespoonfuls into the hot oil. Fry the hushpuppies for about 2 minutes, or until evenly browned, turning often to make sure all sides are evenly browned. Drain on paper towels and serve warm.

chapter 7

MEATS, FISH, AND SEAFOOD

not feed, touch
disturb wildlife.

iolators are subject
 fine and/or arrest

MOUNTAIN FRIED STEAK

serves 4

THIS MELUNGEON RECIPE IS attributed to Josephene Watts Case, who was born in 1870. Josephene advised, "1 pound of steak. Get round steak, because it is the best for this. Pound the steak so that it will be tender for little children and those that don't have good teeth." Here is her recipe as it was given it to me.

———◆——◆———

1 pound round steak, cut into slices

¼ cup flour

1 teaspoon salt

1 tablespoon lard

1 small yellow or white onion, finely chopped

½ cup water

GET the steak pieces and roll them up in the flour and salt. Make sure to cover both sides of the meat good with flour. After that, put the meat into the skillet where the lard is melting and getting hot. Brown the meat good on one side, turn the meat pieces over, and add the onion. Make sure that both sides of the meat are brown. Pour in the water and cover the skillet, and let it simmer till the meat is nice and tender.

NOTE: *I use vegetable shortening instead of lard, and it tastes just fine.*

meat and three

There are small cafés and restaurants all over the southern Appalachian region that serve "meat and three." These places are very popular, serving what's considered good home cookin' or what Granny used to make.

Meat and three is a meal with a meat and three vegetables or sides. The meat can be Salisbury steak, pot roast, fried chicken or such, and the sides are usually some combination of mashed potatoes (and gravy), sweet potatoes (baked or mashed), green beans (with bacon), fried okra, black-eyed peas, macaroni and cheese (heavy on the cheese), corn (on the cob, fried, or creamed), greens (collard or turnip), or skillet apples. Cornbread (with honey butter), biscuits (already buttered), or homemade bread comes with it, as does a tall glass of sweet tea.

Good Brown Gravy

serves 8

I always joke about there being a gravy for everything here in the mountains, but seriously, there is nothing quite as tasty as a good gravy. I've even learned to sop up the gravy on the bottom of the plate with a biscuit. As I understand it, "There ain't no use in lettin' that gravy go to the dawg." Country singer Joe Diffie wrote a song called "Good Brown Gravy" in which he extols its powers, and down at the grocery deli you can order up some homemade brown gravy to ladle over your mashed taters and biscuits while you're resting from all that shopping.

1 tablespoon plus 3 tablespoons (½ stick)
    unsalted butter

1 small yellow onion, diced

1 medium carrot, grated

1 celery heart, diced

2 stalks celery, strings removed and thinly sliced

¼ cup finely chopped fresh parsley

¼ teaspoon dried thyme

½ teaspoon salt

Freshly ground black pepper

¼ cup whole wheat pastry flour

4 cups water

4 cups vegetable stock

IN A SAUTÉ PAN over low heat, add 1 tablespoon of butter and let it melt. Add the onion and let it simmer until they become transparent and browned. Add the carrot, celery, parsley, thyme, salt, and pepper and blend well. Cook until the vegetables brown. Remove from the heat and set aside.

HEAT the remaining 3 tablespoons butter in a heavy saucepan over medium heat. Add the flour and blend well. Stir constantly until the flour browns to a dark color, but be careful not to let it burn. Turn off the heat and add the water and vegetable stock, a little at a time, and rapidly stir until it's blended well. Add the reserved vegetables and blend well.

SIMMER for 2 hours, stirring occasionally, until the gravy is the consistency of whipping cream. Strain to remove the vegetables and serve.

NOTE: *Traditionally this gravy is strained to remove the vegetables, but I see no reason why they can't be left in the gravy. It makes a unique way to serve brown gravy.*

Possum Trot

Possum Trot, Tennessee, was once the home of John Clemens and Jane Lampton Clemens, the parents of Samuel Clemens (a.k.a. author Mark Twain). These days, the Clemens's cabin can be found at the Museum of Appalachia, in Clinton, Tennessee, and Possum Trot is now home to the legendary Highland Regulators. The Highland Regulators, Inc., is an SASS-affiliated shooting club that prides itself on also being a family-oriented facility. The Single Action Shooting Society (SASS) is an international organization created to preserve and promote the sport of Cowboy Action Shooting. The replica of an 1800s southern Appalachian town at Possum Trot is the creation of "Smokin' Joe" Anderson, and the pride of the Regulators. Smokin' Joe is no longer with us, but Possum Trot and the Regulators live on.

POSSUM TROT COWBOY GRAVY

serves 6 to 8

I'VE TASTED SOME "COWBOY" GRAVY BEFORE, but Smokin' Joe's recipe beats them all. I asked him where he learned to cook, and he answered, "As a young boy, I grew up in logging camps. There's not much farming in the hills. All that is grown is a little corn for moonshine. I learned to cook by camping out and in the logging camps." If you prefer thin gravy, cut the corned beef hash in half. This recipe is "good with fried eggs, and biscuits don't hurt," Smokin' Joe told me. Just fill your plate with fried or scrambled eggs, put a nice fresh biscuit in there and ladle Cowboy Gravy over the top of everything. It's just too good to pass up!

6 slices salt bacon, cut into 3-inch pieces

Vegetable oil

1 cup flour (Smokin' Joe preferred White Lily for its texture)

3¾ cups water

1¼ cups 2% milk

2 (15-ounce) cans corned beef hash

Freshly ground black pepper

BROWN the bacon in a large cast-iron skillet over medium heat. Transfer the bacon to a paper towel–lined plate to drain and cool, and pour the bacon drippings out of the skillet. Crumble the cooled bacon and return it to the skillet. Add the oil to the skillet so it is about ⅛-inch deep, and bring it back to medium heat. Slowly add the flour, stirring constantly, until browned.

ADD the water and milk, and stir until the mixture boils and thickens. Add the corned beef hash and continue to stir until blended. Add black pepper to taste. Your gravy should be a nice light brown color. Serve warm.

NOTE: *I'm not fond of too much black pepper, so I put in the smallest amount I can. However, folks who like Cowboy Gravy usually go heavy on the pepper.*

GERMAN BIEROCKS

makes 8

EARLY GERMAN SETTLERS CAME into the southern Appalachian Mountains from Pennsylvania, and their influence on Appalachian culture can be seen throughout the region. The Germans excelled in the art of stonemasonry, and this skill changed the fireplaces, chimneys, and foundations of early mountain cabins. They were also excellent wood-carvers, and their crafts are prized possessions.

A bierock is a dough-wrapped cabbage and meat pie. It seems to have arrived with the Germans who emigrated from Russia. The first time I tasted one was as a child at a German wedding. I've loved them ever since. Church ladies got together to make them for suppers and fund-raisers. Making bierocks is quite a production, but if you only make a few you'll wish that you had made more of them. They freeze well.

FILLING

1 (3- to 4-pound) beef roast

Salt and freshly ground black pepper

2 tablespoons vegetable oil

2 yellow onions, chopped

2 cloves garlic, chopped

1 large head green cabbage, shredded

DOUGH

¾ cup warm water

1 (¼-ounce) package active dry yeast

2 tablespoons sugar

¾ teaspoon salt

1 cup mashed potatoes

2 large eggs

⅓ cup vegetable oil

3 cups all-purpose flour

1½ tablespoons cool water

TO MAKE THE FILLING, rub the roast all over with salt and black pepper. Place the oil in a large skillet over medium heat. Cook the roast until it is richly browned on all sides. Add enough water to cover the roast. Turn the heat to low, cover, and simmer it on the stovetop (or place it in a 325°F oven) until the roast is well done, about 2½ hours. Add more water if necessary to keep ½ inch of water in the pan. When the roast is done, let cool.

REMOVE the meat from the pan. Using two forks, shred the beef and remove any fat, bone, or gristle. Boil the pan drippings until most of the juices evaporate and only fat is left. Set the drippings aside. Coarsely grind the shredded beef in a food processor or meat grinder and set aside.

IN ANOTHER LARGE SKILLET over medium-low heat, add ¼ cup of the reserved drippings and sauté the onion and garlic until the onion is almost golden brown. Add the cabbage and cook, stirring occasionally, until limp and golden, about 1 hour.

Add salt to taste, 2 tablespoons pepper, and the shredded beef to the cabbage mixture, stir to combine, and let stand until cool. (Note: You are using the reserved fat to infuse the meat flavors into the vegetables. You can substitute vegetable oil if you wish.)

TO MAKE THE DOUGH, combine the warm water and yeast in a large bowl and let it stand for 5 minutes, or until bubbly. Add the sugar salt, potatoes, 1 egg, and the vegetable oil and beat, using a stand mixer or a sturdy spoon, until well mixed. Add 1½ cups of the flour and beat for 2 minutes, and then stir in the remaining flour ½ cup at a time. Beat until the dough pulls cleanly from the sides of the bowl, about 10 minutes.

TURN out the dough onto a well-floured surface and knead until smooth and elastic. Add more flour if the dough is too sticky. Place the dough in a greased bowl; turn it over to grease the top. Cover with plastic wrap and let rise in a warm place until doubled, about 1 hour. Punch down and knead on a lightly floured board to expel air bubbles. At this point, dough is ready to use to shape bierocks.

PREHEAT the oven to 375°F. Divide the meat mixture into eight equal portions and set aside. Divide the dough in half, roll out half into an 18-inch square about the thickness of a piecrust, and cut it into quarters. Fill each square with 1 portion of the filling.

MIX the remaining egg and the cool water together to form an egg wash. Brush some egg wash on the edges of each square, and then fold the corners of the dough over the filling to the center and seal them to form a puffy ball. Pinch in the middle to seal. Reserve the remaining egg wash.

PLACE the bierocks, seam side down, about 1 inch apart on ungreased 12 by 15-inch rimmed baking sheets. Cover the baking sheets loosely with plastic wrap and let the dough rise for about 15 minutes, or until puffy.

BRUSH the tops with the remaining egg wash and bake, uncovered, for 15 to 20 minutes, until golden brown. The bierocks can be served hot or at room temperature.

NOTE: *To make ahead of time, cool, cover, and refrigerate the finished bierocks for up to 3 days. Wrap and freeze to store them longer; thaw them still wrapped. To reheat, set the bierocks on ungreased baking sheets and bake them uncovered in a 350°F oven for about 15 minutes, or until hot.*

SOUTHERN BUTTER-CRUSTED CHICKEN

serves 8

THIS IS A SOUL FOOD RECIPE from the southern Appalachian region of northern Alabama. I think this is about as sinful as a fried chicken ought to get. It's absolutely luscious!

---

2 (3-pound) fryer chickens, cut up into serving pieces

Vegetable shortening, for frying

8 tablespoons (1 stick) unsalted butter, melted

6 tablespoons all-purpose flour

1½ teaspoons salt

1 teaspoon paprika

LEFTOVER CORN BREAD GRAVY

8 ounces sliced bacon

2 cups leftover corn bread

½ cup all-purpose flour

2 cups water, plus more if needed

1 to 1½ cups half-and-half, plus more if needed

Salt and freshly ground black pepper

WASH the chicken pieces and pat them dry.

HEAT shortening to a depth of 2 to 3 inches in a deep, heavy skillet over medium heat. Test the heat with a drop of water. If it spatters when it hits the hot oil, it's ready.

IN A BOWL, combine the melted butter, flour, salt, and paprika. Using a pastry brush, coat each piece of chicken completely with the mixture.

PLACE the chicken in the hot oil and fry, turning occasionally, until the coating is golden brown and crispy and the chicken is thoroughly cooked, about 12 minutes on each side. Serve hot.

MAKE THE GRAVY: In a large skillet over medium heat, fry the bacon until crisp. Drain and crumble the bacon and leave the drippings in the skillet.

PUT the crumbled bacon back in the skillet and crumble enough corn bread into the pan to just fill it. Add the flour and stir until the mixture browns. Be careful not to let it burn.

WHEN the mixture is browned, slowly add the water and half-and-half until the mixture forms a gravy, adding more water or half-and-half if necessary. Season to taste with salt and pepper and serve hot.

MEAT LOAF
serves 4 to 6

THIS RECIPE FROM THE 1869 Shaker Tavern Bed & Breakfast in South Union, Kentucky, is another delicious addition to this book. The tavern presents a "Shaker Breakfast" once each year, when they cook the menus from old Shaker journals; and in the spring they have a "Railroad Luncheon," presenting menus from old railroad hotels. Both sound like fun to me. For more on the tavern, see page 79.

Meat loaf has been a favorite of mine since childhood, and although it may not be considered gourmet food by many, it's certainly a dish that can be served at either the kitchen table or the dining room table. It all depends on how you present it. My favorite way to eat it is the next day in a cold sandwich with lettuce, a slice of tomato, and a little mayonnaise. Be sure not to cover the meat loaf before baking it. While you might think it would burn by being cooked for so long, it doesn't. The toppings make a delicate crust.

LOAF

⅔ cup saltine cracker crumbs (I like to use whole wheat saltine crumbs)

1 cup milk

¼ cup chopped yellow onion

1 teaspoon salt

Pinch of freshly ground black pepper

1 tablespoon (or less) ground dried sage

1½ pounds lean ground beef

TOPPING

6 tablespoons firmly packed brown sugar

1 cup ketchup

1 tablespoon dry mustard

PREHEAT the oven to 350°F.

PLACE the cracker crumbs in a large bowl, pour the milk over the crumbs, and stir to moisten them. Add the chopped onion, salt, pepper, and sage and blend well. Mix in the ground beef. Form the mixture into a loaf and place it in a 7 by 9-inch baking dish.

TO MAKE THE TOPPING, mix the brown sugar, ketchup, and dry mustard together in a small bowl and pour it over the top of the meat loaf.

BAKE the meat loaf, uncovered, for 1½ hours, or until the top of the loaf has a nice crust. Let cool

CHICKEN NOODLE CASSEROLE

serves 12 to 14

BUILT ON AN OLD FAMILY FARM, the Blue Mountain Mist Country Inn in Sevierville, Tennessee, has been welcoming folks for twenty years. Do you remember going to your mam-maw's (Appalachian for "grandmother") for supper and you, Mam-Maw, and Paw-Paw (Grandfather) sat down to something like a chicken noodle casserole, some biscuits, greens, and maybe pudding for dessert? This recipe is classically good, and whether you serve it to family or friends, you are sure to hear a story about what it reminds them of. That's what makes southern Appalachian food comfort food.

---

8 boneless, skinless chicken breasts

1 (26-ounce) carton chicken broth

1 (12-ounce) package extra-wide egg noodles

2 tablespoons unsalted butter

2 medium white onions, chopped

2 green bell peppers, seeded and finely chopped

1 (4-ounce) jar pimientos, drained

2 cups grated sharp cheddar cheese (reserve ¼ cup)

Salt and freshly ground black pepper

2 (10¾-ounce) cans cream of chicken soup

PLACE the chicken breasts in a large saucepan over medium heat. Cover them with water and bring to a low boil. Boil until the chicken is just done, about 20 minutes. The pieces should be evenly white. Be careful not to overcook. Transfer to a plate to cool.

REDUCE the heat to low, add the chicken broth and noodles to the saucepan, and cook them according to the package directions.

WHILE the noodles are cooking, heat the butter in a skillet over medium-low heat and sauté the onions and peppers until tender.

DRAIN the cooked noodles and set them aside. Cut the cooled chicken into bite-size cubes.

PREHEAT the oven to 350°F and lightly butter or spray a large baking dish. Place enough cooked noodles in the baking dish to completely cover the bottom in a thin layer. Top the noodles with enough chicken to cover the noodles. Cover the chicken with enough sautéed onions and peppers to cover, add a sprinkling of pimientos, and then top it with a layer of cheese. Season with salt and pepper. Repeat the layering until the dish is almost full. (Note: The number of layers depends on how thick or thin you make them, it's up to you.)

MIX the cream of chicken soup with 1 cup of water and pour the mixture evenly over the casserole. Evenly sprinkle the reserved ¼ cup cheese over the top. Bake the casserole for 30 to 40 minutes, until it is bubbling and the cheese is thoroughly melted. Serve immediately.

BURGOO

makes 1 gallon

BURGOO IS A SAVORY STEW made from a variety of ingredients and traces its roots to the early Irish settlers in the mountains. Burgoo traditionally included whatever meats and vegetables were available, usually venison, squirrel, opossum, or game birds. Modern burgoo recipes use pork, chicken, beef, or mutton. There are as many different ways to make burgoo as there are people who make it. It's often cooked in large iron kettles outdoors over an open fire. Cooking can take as long as thirty hours, and the flavor improves with age.

FOR DAY ONE

4 quarts water

1 (5-pound) roasting chicken

1 pound beef stew meat

1 pound veal stew meat

4 large beef bones

1 chopped scallion

2 green bell peppers, seeded and finely chopped

1 medium turnip, diced

FOR DAY TWO

2 cups fresh butter beans, shelled

10 medium tomatoes, peeled and chopped

2 cups thinly sliced celery

2 cups finely chopped green cabbage

1 (10-ounce) can tomato puree

6 ears fresh corn on the cob

2 cups thinly sliced carrots

2 cups chopped yellow or white onions

2 cups thinly sliced fresh okra

1 cup chopped fresh parsley, plus more for garnish

½ lemon, seeded

1 tablespoon freshly squeezed lemon juice

1 tablespoon Worcestershire sauce

1 tablespoon sugar

1 dried red pepper pod

¼ cup salt

1½ teaspoons coarsely ground black pepper

½ teaspoon cayenne pepper

ON DAY ONE, in a roasting pan, combine the water, chicken, beef stew meat, veal stew meat, beef bones, scallion, bell pepper, and turnip. Bring to a boil, and then turn the heat down to simmer. Cover and simmer for 4 hours. Let cool, and then strain and reserve the broth. Remove the skin and bones from the chicken and finely chop the chicken and stew meat. Remove and discard the beef bones. Return the chopped meat to the cooled stock and refrigerate it overnight.

ON DAY TWO, lift off half of the fat from the top of the stock and return the stock and the meat to the stove over medium-low heat. Add the butter beans, tomatoes, celery, cabbage, and tomato puree and cook for 1 hour, until thick.

PREHEAT the oven to 300°F.

IN A BOWL, scrape the corncobs to remove the kernels. Add the corn to the pot, along with the carrots, onions, okra, parsley, lemon, lemon juice, Worcestershire sauce, sugar, red pepper pod, salt, cayenne pepper, and black pepper. Stir to blend, and cook, uncovered, in the oven for 2 hours, or until the burgoo is the consistency of a thick stew. Serve hot.

superstitions

It's very bad luck to bathe on your wedding day.

To keep a witch out of your house, lay a broom across the doorstep.

A snakeskin bag with a toad's eye inside will keep away ghosts.

If a girl takes the last piece of bread off a plate, she will be an old maid.

Headache remedy: Put a handful of salt on your head.

There will be rain if your nose itches.

There will be rain if a rooster crows at night.

A bad winter is coming if onions grow more layers.

SPICED CRANBERRY
PORK ROAST

serves 4 to 6

THE MOMENT YOU ARRIVE at the Calico Inn in Sevierville, Tennessee, you can see why so many people come back time and again. It's an authentic log cabin with a view of Mount LeConte, the third highest peak in the Great Smoky Mountains. The mountain was named after a member of the LeConte family, but just which member is a matter for debate. It was measured in the 1850s but not much went on up there until the 1920s, when an enthusiastic hiker and explorer spent much of his time in the mountains exploring trails and leading groups into the area. In 1924, he led an expedition of Washington dignitaries up onto Mount LeConte, where they spent the night. They experienced the rugged beauty and raw nature of the place, and about ten years later, Mount LeConte was protected and included as part of the Great Smoky Mountains National Park. This recipe is one of the many delicious dishes served at the inn. Cranberry is one of my favorite flavors, and its addition to this pork roast makes a lovely dish.

---

1 (2 ½- to 3-pound) boneless rolled pork loin roast

1 (16-ounce) can jellied whole cranberry sauce

½ cup sugar

1 teaspoon dry mustard

¼ teaspoon ground cloves

2 tablespoons cold water

2 tablespoons cornstarch

Salt

PREHEAT the oven to 250°F. Place the roast in a baking pan.

IN A BOWL, mash together the cranberry sauce, sugar, dry mustard, and cloves.

POUR the mixture over the roast and cover the pan. Cook for 6 to 8 hours, until the roast is thoroughly cooked and tender.

REMOVE the roast from the oven, transfer it to a cutting board, and pour the juices into a saucepan. Skim off the fat. Bring the pan juices to a boil over medium-high heat. In a small bowl, combine the water and cornstarch to form a paste. Slowly stir the paste into the pan juices and cook, stirring, until thickened. Add salt to taste.

SLICE the roast and serve it with the sauce spooned over the top.

NOTE: *To make the roast in a slow cooker, place the roast in the cooker and turn the heat to low. Make the sauce as directed above and pour it over the roast. Cover and cook on low for 6 to 8 hours.*

COUNTRY HAM

serves ½ pound per person

THE HAMS PURCHASED IN A GROCERY are usually sugar cured, and the label will say "water added." These hams are ready for baking. Country hams, on the other hand, are salt cured. They should look dehydrated and wrinkled, and they need preparation before baking.

---

1 country ham

PLACE the country ham in the bottom of a large pot and fill it with water. Then place the pot in the refrigerator and let it sit for 12 to 24 hours.

REMOVE the ham, pour out the water, and clean the pot. Put the ham back in the pot and fill it with water. Place the pot on the stove and bring the water to a near boil over medium heat, and then turn the heat to low and cook for several hours at a simmer until the ham is completely tender.

PREHEAT the oven to 350°F. Remove the ham from the cooking water and remove and discard the rind. It is not edible. Put the ham in a baking pan and bake it until it is hot. Slice it and serve it with plenty of redeye gravy (recipe on page 32).

hogs

Appalachian Mountain farmers once raised millions of swine each year. Because hogs were so easy to care for, pork became the main source of protein for the southern Appalachian mountain people. Hogs are hardy, independent animals, capable of finding their own food and defending themselves against predators. This made them the perfect mountain livestock. During the summer months, hogs were allowed to roam free and feed on forest foods like chestnuts and roots, which produced a fat hog at no expense to the farmer. If a farmer's sow met up with a neighbor's boar, the resulting piglets were a bonus. It must be that not all of those hogs returned home, though, because to this day there are wild boar and hogs roaming all over the mountains.

RICK'S "EASY FIXINS" PARTY HAM

serves 10 to 12

MY NEIGHBOR RICK LOVES TO COOK. I was over there after dinner one night having coffee and catching up on the news when I spotted this ham sitting on the kitchen counter. Lori (that's Mrs. Rick) offered me some and I couldn't resist. It looked so good. I asked how Rick had cooked it and Lori said, "It's so simple, but it's really good." I had to agree. This simple recipe is absolutely delicious! If you make it according to Rick's directions, the meat just falls off the bone.

1 (8-pound) bone-in ham

1¼ cups pineapple juice

1 (15¼-ounce) can fruit cocktail in juice

½ cup firmly packed brown sugar

¼ cup water

PLACE an oven rack in the middle position in the oven and preheat the oven to 300°F.

USING a carving knife, slice the ham halfway down to the bone. Place the ham in a baking pan and pour the pineapple juice over it. Pour the fruit cocktail on top. Stir together the brown sugar and water and pour it over the top of everything.

COOK the ham for 5 hours, or until it's slightly browned and the meat easily separates from the bone. It's is delicious served hot or cold.

PORK CHOPS, SOUTHERN-STYLE

serves 8

THERE ISN'T JUST ONE TYPE of southern-style pork chop. What makes a chop "southern" is the touch of sweetness. I like this recipe because it's simple and delicious.

2 tablespoons vegetable shortening

8 (4-ounce) boneless center-cut pork loin chops, about ½ inch thick

⅛ teaspoon salt

½ teaspoon ground dried sage

4 Granny Smith apples, cored and sliced into rings about ¼ inch thick

¼ cup firmly packed brown sugar

2 tablespoons all-purpose flour

1 cup hot water

1 tablespoon cider vinegar

½ cup raisins

PREHEAT the oven to 350°F. Heat the shortening in a large skillet over medium heat and brown the pork chops well on both sides.

TRANSFER the chops to a baking dish, sprinkle them with the salt and sage, and top them with the apple rings. Sprinkle the brown sugar over the tops of the apples.

ADD THE FLOUR to the fat in the skillet and blend well. Stir in the water and vinegar and cook until the mixture thickens. Add the raisins, stirring to blend, and then pour the mixture over the chops.

BAKE, uncovered, for 1 hour. Serve immediately.

Larry had a mess of pigs up on his place. One day the county agent was up there talking to him and noticed that there was no fence. "How you keep all these pigs from leaving?" the agent asked. Larry looked him straight in the eye and said, "I showed 'em a map of my land."

PULLED PORK BARBECUE

serves 8 to 10

TASTY, TASTY, TASTY! Pulled pork barbecue restaurants in southern Appalachia serve their meat two ways: (1) plopped over an open roll as a sandwich, or (2) as a main meat with greens, sweet potatoes, and biscuits. And they always include a little extra barbecue sauce (recipe follows) on the side.

———— ◆–◆ ————

1 (2-pound) pork shoulder roast

1 large yellow or white onion, quartered and sliced

1 tablespoon garlic powder

Salt and freshly ground black pepper

1 cup barbecue sauce (your favorite, or the recipe that follows)

½ cup white vinegar

BARBECUE SAUCE

3 tablespoons bacon drippings

⅓ cup chopped yellow or white onion

⅓ cup chopped red bell pepper

⅓ cup chopped celery

1 small clove garlic, minced

½ cup raisins

⅓ cup tomato sauce

1 tablespoon cider vinegar

¼ teaspoon salt

Pinch of freshly ground black pepper

1 tablespoon all-purpose flour

1 cup water

PLACE the pork in a slow cooker and add the sliced onion and garlic powder.

COVER and cook on low for 9 to 11 hours, or until very tender and shreddable.

REMOVE the roast from the cooker and allow it to cool. Drain off the juices from the cooker and discard them. When the roast is cool enough to handle, remove any bones and fat and, using your fingers and a fork, shred the meat until the entire roast is torn apart.

RETURN the meat to the cooker and add the barbecue sauce and vinegar, and season with the salt and pepper. Turn the heat to high and cooking for 1 more hour. Serve hot.

MAKE THE SAUCE: In a large saucepan over medium heat, combine the drippings, onion, bell pepper, celery, and garlic and sauté for 5 minutes. Reduce the heat to a simmer. Add the raisins, tomato sauce, vinegar, salt, and black pepper and simmer for 20 minutes, stirring occasionally.

LET the sauce cool a little, and then puree it in a blender or food processor until smooth. Return the sauce to the saucepan over medium heat. Combine the flour with the water and stir to form a paste. Add it to the sauce and stir until the sauce comes to a boil and thickens, about 20 minutes. Refrigerate until ready to use.

ROAST CRISPED-SKIN TURKEY

serves 10 to 12

LOCATED IN MARS HILL, just north of Asheville, North Carolina, Ponder Cove Inn sits on 91 wonderfully peaceful acres in the Blue Ridge Mountains. Folks bring their dogs along with them, and everyone has a good time. The owners are talented people who have been featured in magazines and on television specials. Martha loves to cook and combines country cooking with a sophisticated twist. While you're there you can visit husband Gary Rawlins in his woodworking shop. Trained in England, master craftsman Gary creates beautiful, museum-quality, hand-hewn furniture. This recipe from them is extremely good and a nice change for turkey lovers.

---

4 cups kosher salt, or 2 cups table salt

2 gallons cold water

1 (12- to 14-pound) fresh or defrosted frozen turkey,
    rinsed and giblets removed

1 stalk celery, coarsely chopped

2 medium yellow onions, coarsely chopped

1 medium carrot, coarsely chopped

   4 sprigs thyme

6 tablespoons unsalted butter, melted

DISSOLVE the salt in the cold water in a large stockpot. Add the turkey and refrigerate for 4 to 6 hours. You can also refrigerate it overnight, but if you do, cut the amount of salt in half.

REMOVE the turkey from the salt water, rinse it well under cool running water, and pat it dry inside and out with paper towels. Place the turkey breast side up on a flat wire rack set over a rimmed baking sheet or in a roasting pan and refrigerate it, uncovered, for 8 to 24 hours.

PLACE the oven rack in the lowest position in the oven and preheat the oven to 400°F.

DIVIDE the celery, onions, and carrot into 3 equal portions. Toss one-third of the vegetables with 2 sprigs of the thyme and 1 tablespoon of the butter in a medium bowl, then fill the turkey cavity with the mixture. Tuck the wings behind the back and truss the turkey. Scatter the remaining two-thirds of the celery, onions, carrot, and the remaining 2 sprigs thyme in a shallow roasting pan and pour 1 cup of water over them. Brush the turkey breast and back with some of the remaining butter, then set it breast side down on an aluminum foil–lined V-shaped rack.

ROAST the turkey for 45 minutes, and then remove it from the oven and brush the back again with butter. Using oven mitts, rotate the turkey so that one leg/wing side faces up. If the liquid in the bottom of the pan has evaporated, add ½ cup water. Roast for 15 minutes longer, and then remove the roasting pan, brush the turkey again with butter, flip it to other leg/wing side, and roast for 15 minutes longer.

Remove the turkey, brush it with butter again, and flip it so that the breast side faces up.

ROAST the turkey for 30 to 45 minutes longer, until the thickest part of the breast registers 165°F on an instant-read thermometer and the thickest part of the thigh registers 170° to175°F. Transfer the turkey to a carving board and let it rest for 20 to 30 minutes before carving.

Sausage and Corn Bread Dressing
serves 8

Sausage and cornbread dressing is a classic southern tradition. This recipe will fill a 10- to 14-pound turkey.

1 tablespoon plus 5 tablespoons unsalted butter

1 pound spicy bulk sausage

2 medium sweet onions, chopped

4 stalks celery, thinly sliced

6 cups soft bread crumbs, plus more if needed

6 cups crumbled corn bread

1 cup chicken broth

1 teaspoon rubbed dried sage

½ teaspoon dried thyme

¼ teaspoon dried marjoram

¼ teaspoon freshly ground black pepper

1 large egg, lightly beaten

Sea salt or kosher salt

PREHEAT the oven to 350°F and lightly grease or butter a 9 by 13-inch broiler-proof baking dish.

MELT 1 tablespoon of the butter in a large skillet over medium heat. Add the

SAUSAGE and cook completely through, crumbling it as it cooks. Drain the sausage in a colander and set it aside. Remove all but 2 tablespoons of the drippings from the skillet, add the onions and celery, and cook until tender. Transfer the mixture to a bowl.

IN A SEPARATE LARGE BOWL, combine the bread crumbs and corn bread and toss to blend. Add the sausage and onion-celery mixture and blend well.

IN ANOTHER BOWL, combine the chicken broth, sage, thyme, marjoram, pepper, and egg and beat until well blended. Pour the broth mixture over the bread mixture and stir until the bread is well moistened. If the mixture is too mushy, add more bread crumbs.

MELT the remaining 5 tablespoons butter in a saucepan and stir it into the bread mixture. Taste and season with salt.

PRESS the mixture into the prepared baking dish and cover it with aluminum foil. Bake for 40 minutes, and then uncover the dish and place it under the broiler to brown the top. Serve hot.

NOTE: *If using this recipe to stuff the bird, rub the inside cavity of the bird lightly with sea salt or kosher salt before stuffing it. Do not use too much salt, as a little goes a long way here and the flavor will go all through the meat and stuffing.*

TROUT CAKES
serves 6 (makes 24)

THE TROUTDALE DINING ROOM in Bristol, Tennessee, is a southern Appalachian regional jewel located in an elegant 1850 Victorian house. A five-star restaurant, it was selected as one of America's Outstanding Restaurants in both the twentieth and twenty-first centuries by the International Restaurant and Hospitality Rating Bureau. These trout cakes can be presented in a variety of ways just by adding or subtracting ingredients. This particular version is Cajun-style, and it's absolutely delicious. Serve them for dinner with the sauce that follows, or serve them for a luncheon. You can also reduce the size of the cake and use them as an appetizer without the sauce.

---

1 pound cooked trout (about 5 fillets)

1 red bell pepper, seeded and finely chopped

2 tablespoons plus 1 tablespoon olive oil

1 green bell pepper, seeded and diced

2 shallots, diced

2 cloves garlic

1 cup dry seasoned bread crumbs

2 large eggs

1½ tablespoons Creole mustard

1 tablespoon mayonnaise

1 tablespoon freshly squeezed lemon juice

Salt and freshly ground black pepper

2 tablespoons water

Vegetable oil, for frying

PREHEAT the oven to 375°F.

TO PREPARE THE TROUT, lightly spray or grease a baking pan and lay the fillets skin side down in the pan. Bake for 10 to 12 minutes. Remove the pan from the oven and, using a fork, remove the meat from the skin. Place it in a large bowl and set aside.

TO ROAST the red pepper, turn the oven temperature to 400°F. Put the chopped pepper pieces in a baking dish with 2 tablespoons of the olive oil and bake for 25 to 30 minutes, until the pieces are tender and slightly browned.

WHILE the pepper is roasting, sauté the green pepper and the shallots in the remaining 1 tablespoon olive oil and set aside.

REMOVE the red pepper from the oven and add it to the trout, along with the green pepper and shallots, garlic, ¼ cup of the bread crumbs, 1 egg, the mustard, mayonnaise, lemon juice, salt, and pepper, and mix well. In a small bowl, mix the remaining egg and the water. Beat lightly with a fork to blend. To another bowl, add the remaining ¾ cup bread crumbs.

FORM the trout mixture into cakes the size of a silver dollar. Dip each trout cake into the egg wash, then dredge it in the bread crumbs. Completely cover each trout cake with a light coating of bread crumbs. Place them on a plate while you prepare the next step.

PREHEAT the oven to 350°F. Heat ¼ inch of vegetable oil in a large sauté pan over medium-low heat. Sauté the trout cakes until golden brown, about 30 seconds on each side. Place the trout cakes in a large baking dish and bake for 10 minutes, or until hot throughout. Serve immediately.

Cajun Rémoulade Sauce
serves 6

This sauce is not part of the original recipe, but the chef at the Troutdale suggested to me that it would be a nice accompaniment.

1 cup mayonnaise

¼ cup chili sauce

2 tablespoons Creole or dark mustard

2 tablespoons extra-virgin olive oil

1 tablespoon Cajun hot sauce (use much less if it's too hot for you)

2 tablespoons freshly squeezed lemon juice

1 teaspoon Worcestershire sauce

4 medium scallions, finely chopped (white and green parts)

2 tablespoons finely chopped fresh parsley

2 tablespoons finely chopped green olives

2 tablespoons minced celery

1 teaspoon capers, chopped (optional)

1 clove garlic, minced

Salt

½ teaspoon freshly ground black pepper

IN A BOWL, combine the mayonnaise, chili sauce, mustard, olive oil, hot sauce, lemon juice, and Worcestershire sauce. Stir in the scallions, parsley, olives, celery, capers, and garlic. Taste and season with salt and pepper. Cover and refrigerate until ready to serve.

alligator hunting in the mountains

A group of local folks were gathered at the tables in the back when I arrived at the gas station to fill up my car. Miss Julia, bless her heart, was in the center entertaining the gentlemen with her stories, and no one was seeming to mind that she tells the same stories over and over again, each time a bit grander than before. "How ya be, Miss Julia?" I asked as I poured a fountain drink and joined the others.

Everyone was all abuzz and laughing when I sat down. She asked me where a certain person was and I said I didn't know and she said, "I want him to go hunting with me tomorrow." Now, Miss Julia is of a certain age, and the thought of her hunting made me kind of nervous. I pictured a bear turning and chasing her around in circles. Just the week before she had told me how she had killed a Black Racer snake because she didn't want to have to run into it in her back field. "What are you hunting?" I asked. "Alligator!" she replied with a big grin. "That Miss Julia," the boy behind the deli counter mumbled as he shook his head. "Now you hesh up," Miss Julia told him with a smile. "Miss Julia, you want something to eat?" he asked her. She shook her head and said that she was fine. I sat there waiting for the story, whatever it was going to be, laughed, and said, "Okay Miss Julia, I'm listening."

"You didn't hear?" she asked. I shook my head no. "Well, they got a gator in the Little Pigeon." She went on with the story. "This afternoon, some kids was fishin' on the Pigeon and they seen the gator. So they run over to the police and tell them what they seen right there in Pigeon Forge." Now the Little Pigeon River runs right through Pigeon Forge, which is just a speck of a place, but since it's the birthplace of Dolly Parton, there are tourists everywhere and the police are everywhere, too. The kids must have been down river from the Old Mill, and the gator must have slipped over the spillway. "So," she continued, "there was two policemen and they tried to catch the gator by getting a rope around its neck and pulling on him. The rope broke and that old gator swam away as fast as he could." She started laughing, and I was wondering how they would get that gator into a squad car when she said, "That's why I'm going gator shooting tomorrow." I stated the obvious, that someone must have gone to Florida and brought back a baby gator and, when it got too big, put it in the river. She leaned over close and, using her hand to gesture, pointed toward old Hank. "He used to have a gator up there," she said.

"You causin' trouble, woman?" Hank said to me with a big grin on his face. "You ain't talkin' politics, is ya?" he said with a laugh. Miss Julia glared at him and said, "Where's that gator you had up thar?" "He died," Hank replied. "Well, he's sure gonna be dead after I find him," Miss Julia said. "Young 'uns play in that river," she added. Julia is mad at Hank because he goes dancing on Saturday nights. "He ought to be home reading his Bible," she says. "Yes, ma'am, I'm gonna git me a gator," she told us. As for me, I've been watching to see if Miss Julia starts wearing alligator shoes.

MARINATED GRILLED SALMON

serves 4

THIS IS A FAVORITE DISH in many southern restaurants. I first tasted it in Nashville, Tennessee, and I've since found it here in the mountains. Salmon by itself is lovely, but this marinated salmon is incredible. You'll want to savor every bite.

2 teaspoons unsalted butter, melted

1 clove garlic, mashed

¼ cup firmly packed brown sugar

¾ cup bourbon

¼ cup brown mustard

¼ teaspoon freshly ground black pepper

4 (8-ounce) salmon fillets

IN A MEDIUM BOWL, whisk together the butter, garlic, brown sugar, bourbon, mustard, and pepper.

PLACE the salmon in a shallow baking dish and cover it with the marinade. Cover the dish and let it sit in the refrigerator for at least 1 hour. It's much better if marinated for 2 to 3 hours.

SPRAY the grill grate and build a hot fire in the grill. Place the salmon on the hot grill and cook for about 5 minutes on each side, or until it flakes and becomes lighter in color. Serve hot.

KENTUCKY HOT BROWN

serves 2

THIS SANDWICH IS A RICH AND TASTY KENTUCKY TRADITION. It originated at the Brown Hotel in Louisville in 1923, and it's been a favorite ever since. The original recipe was made with bread, turkey, bacon, and pimento browned under a broiler and covered with Mornay sauce. Southern cooks like to experiment, and this version of the recipe is very good.

————————————

1½ teaspoons unsalted butter

3 tablespoons all-purpose flour

1½ cups milk

¼ cup grated Parmesan cheese

Southern hot sauce (can use Tabasco)

1 egg yolk

1 cup grated Colby cheese

4 slices bread, toasted on both sides

4 slices cooked turkey breast, cut in half diagonally

4 slices tomato, cut in half diagonally

8 slices bacon, cooked until crispy

IN A LARGE, heavy saucepan over medium-low heat, melt the butter. Add the flour and stir until blended and smooth. Slowly add the milk and cook until the sauce thickens. Add the Parmesan cheese, stirring to blend. Add a few dashes of hot sauce to taste, blend well, and remove the pan from the heat.

REMOVE ½ cup of the sauce and beat the egg yolk into it. Return the egg mixture to the sauce in the pan and stir to blend, and then mix in the Colby cheese.

PREHEAT the oven to 400°F.

TO MAKE THE SANDWICH, cut each toasted bread piece in half diagonally and place the triangles on ovenproof plates. Place turkey slices on top of each toast, then spoon all of the sauce evenly over the turkey. Place a tomato slice on top, followed by two slices of bacon.

BAKE for 10 to 15 minutes, or until the cheese bubbles. Serve hot.

music in the mountains

Most of the authentic musical genres in America originated in the South. Bluegrass, country music, the blues, rock-a-billy, rock and roll, folk music, and gospel come from basic roots in this area. As I write this from my mountain "holler," Carl, my neighbor up the way, is playing music with a few friends and it's ringing through the trees and down the mountain. They're playing a modernized version of an old classic and the electric guitar licks are dancing around the melody. Sound travels through a holler like a telephone line and I can hear them laughing and talking, too. It's like that here. Music is as much a part of southern Appalachian life as getting up in the morning.

The ancient Cherokee morning song greets the new day:

We n' de ya ho, We n' de ya ho,
We n' de ya, We n' de ya, Ho ho ho ho,
He ya ho, He ya ho, Ya ya ya
(I am of the Great Spirit. It is so.)

Black Africans, who came early to the mountains, brought their musical traditions and instruments with them. One African instrument, called a griot, was the basis for the American banjo. The music of the Melungeons had some Turkish and Romany roots, and the Scotch-Irish and Scandinavians had their traditional folk music. And so it began. The evolution of what we now call country music, bluegrass, the blues, and rock-a-billy could only have happened here. The meshing of cultures and the adaptation of musical traditions, coupled with the shared struggle for survival, formed the groundwork for southern Appalachian music.

BAKED CATFISH WITH PECANS AND SPICY BUTTER SAUCE

serves 4

YOU CAN SUBSTITUTE ANY white-fleshed fish for the catfish. Whether you catch your own or use farmed catfish (which I recommend), this is a very nice way to serve the fish.

FISH

4 (6-ounce) catfish fillets

Salt and freshly ground black pepper

¾ cup pecans

1 cup bread crumbs

2 tablespoons unsalted butter, melted

1 tablespoon brown mustard

¼ cup grated Parmesan cheese

1 teaspoon dried dill

1 tablespoon dried parsley

Olive oil, for drizzling

SPICY BUTTER SAUCE

¾ cup (1½ sticks) unsalted butter

2 tablespoons freshly squeezed lemon juice

1 teaspoon Worcestershire sauce

1 teaspoon brown mustard

3 tablespoons mild chili sauce

Lemon wedges, for garnish

PREHEAT the oven to 375°F and butter or spray a 9 by 13 by 2-inch broiler-proof baking dish. Place the fish in the dish and sprinkle it with salt and pepper.

GRIND the pecans in a blender or food processor until finely chopped. In a medium bowl, combine the bread crumbs and pecans. Add the butter, mustard, cheese, dill, and parsley and mix until well combined. Pat down the crumbs onto the top of each fillet, then drizzle with olive oil.

BAKE for 15 minutes, or until the fish is done. While the fish is baking, make the sauce by melting the butter in a saucepan over medium-low heat. Stir in the lemon juice, Worcestershire sauce, mustard, and chili sauce. Heat just until bubbly.

IF DESIRED, place the baked fish under the broiler to brown the crust a little more. Serve immediately with spicy butter sauce and lemon wedges.

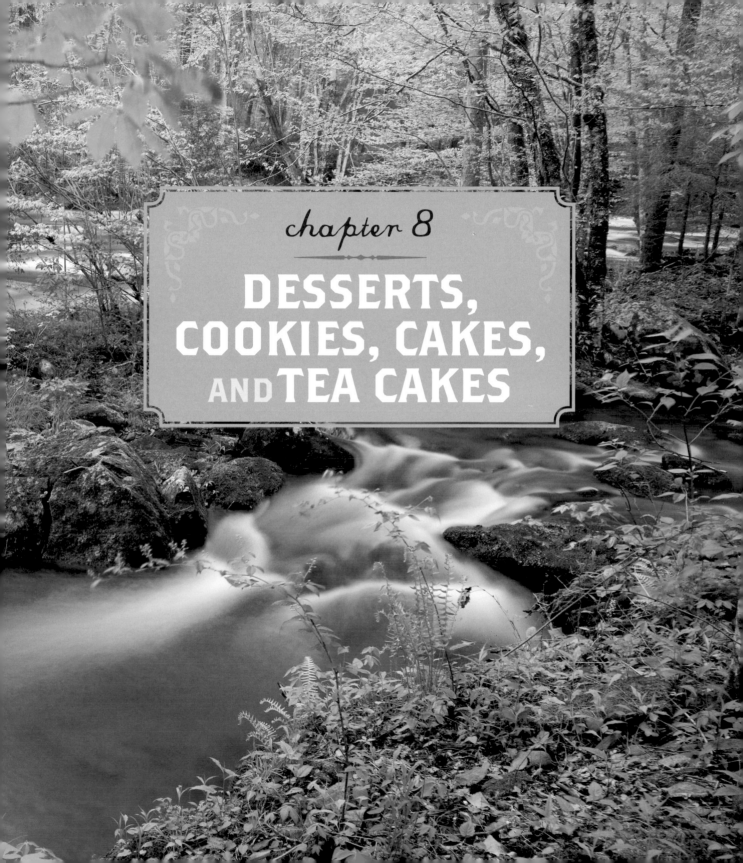

chapter 8

DESSERTS, COOKIES, CAKES, and TEA CAKES

PECAN-BANANA CAKE

makes one 9-inch layer cake

A HISTORIC 1930S SMOKY MOUNTAIN LODGE, Laurel Springs Lodge Bed and Breakfast, in Gatlinburg, Tennessee, has welcomed guests for some seventy years. The mountains, the friendly Appalachian people, the food, and the river just 100 feet behind the lodge, where folks fish for mountain trout, all keep people coming back The quaint guest rooms with lace-curtained windows looking out onto the river and forest are charmingly welcoming. This delicious cake from the lodge will have people coming back for seconds.

CAKE

½ cup vegetable shortening

1½ cups granulated sugar

2 large eggs

¾ cup buttermilk

2 cups all-purpose flour

1 teaspoon baking soda

1 teaspoon baking powder

½ teaspoon salt

2 large ripe bananas, mashed

1 cup chopped pecans

1 teaspoon vanilla extract

CREAM CHEESE FROSTING

3 ounces cream cheese, at room temperature

4 tablespoons (½ stick) unsalted butter,
    at room temperature

1½ teaspoons milk

2 cups confectioners' sugar

1 teaspoon vanilla extract

Fresh strawberries, hulled and halved, for garnish

PREHEAT the oven to 350°F and lightly grease and flour two 9-inch round cake pans.

TO MAKE THE CAKE, cream together the shortening and granulated sugar in a large bowl. Beat in the eggs and buttermilk. Sift the flour, baking soda, baking powder, and salt together into the buttermilk mixture and blend well. Add the bananas, pecans, and vanilla and blend until smooth and well combined.

POUR the batter into the prepared cake pans and bake for 30 minutes, or until a toothpick inserted in the center of each cake comes out clean. Let the cakes cool in the pans on a wire rack for 30 minutes.

WHILE the cakes are cooling, make the frosting. Beat the cream cheese, butter, milk, confectioners' sugar, and vanilla in the bowl of a stand mixer on medium speed until smooth.

GENTLY invert the cake pans and remove the cakes from the pans. Place one of the rounds on a serving plate and spread to the edge with a thin layer of frosting (about ⅛ inch thick). Place the second layer on top of the first layer and frost as usual. Garnish with fresh strawberry halves.

KENTUCKY BOURBON CAKE

makes 1 Bundt cake

THIS CAKE IS STARTED THE DAY BEFORE and is a great after-dinner or special-occasion cake for grownups; and it's even better if you let it "age" for a few days in the refrigerator. Store leftover cake in a tightly covered container.

FOR DAY ONE

1 cup maraschino cherries, drained and halved

1 cup raisins

1 cup chopped dried dates

2 cups bourbon

FOR DAY TWO

1½ cups (3 sticks) unsalted butter, at room temperature

2 cups granulated sugar

1 cup firmly packed brown sugar

6 large eggs, separated

½ cup plus 4½ cups all-purpose flour

1½ cups chopped walnuts or pecans

1½ teaspoons ground nutmeg

1 teaspoon baking powder

ON DAY ONE, combine the cherries, raisins, dates, and bourbon in a large bowl. Cover the bowl and let the mixture sit overnight.

ON DAY TWO, preheat the oven to 275°F and lightly grease and flour a 10-inch Bundt or other tube-shaped pan. Lightly trace the shape of the bottom of the pan on waxed paper, cut out the circle, and use it to line the bottom of the pan. Lightly grease the waxed paper.

USING a stand mixer, cream together the butter, granulated sugar, and brown sugar on medium speed until light and fluffy. Add the egg yolks and beat well. Using a slotted spoon, remove the fruit from the liquid and gently stir it into the egg mixture.

COMBINE ½ cup of the flour with the chopped nuts and stir until all of the nuts are coated. Set aside.

SLOWLY add the remaining 4½ cups flour to the batter until thoroughly combined. Stir in the nutmeg and baking powder.

IN A MEDIUM BOWL with clean beaters, beat the egg whites until peaks form, and then gently fold them into the batter. Gently fold in the floured nuts.

POUR the batter into the prepared pan and bake for 3 to 3½ hours, until a skewer or table knife inserted into the cake comes out clean. Let the cake cool completely on a wire rack, and then invert it onto a serving platter, remove the waxed paper, slice, and serve.

TENNESSEE BLACK WALNUT CAKE

makes 1 Bundt cake

THIS SPECIAL-OCCASION CAKE IS A SOUTHERN FAVORITE and is often served for holiday dinners. A very old recipe, this cake has seen a few variations. Black walnut trees are abundant in the southern Appalachian forests, and the early settlers gathered the nuts for food. Folks tell stories of how they accompanied a mother or grandmother to gather the nuts and then went back home and helped her make this cake. Because the Bundt pan was invented in the 1950s, chances are that the original black walnut cakes were baked in common baking dishes.

CAKE

1 cup all-purpose flour

1 teaspoon salt

1 teaspoon baking powder

1 teaspoon ground cinnamon

½ teaspoon ground nutmeg

¼ teaspoon ground allspice

7 large eggs, separated

¼ tablespoon cream of tartar

½ cup light corn syrup

½ cup light molasses

1 teaspoon vanilla extract

¾ cup finely chopped black walnuts

WALNUT FROSTING

1 cup heavy whipping cream

¾ cup sifted confectioners' sugar

½ teaspoon ground cinnamon

¼ teaspoon salt

Black walnuts, halved, for garnish

PREHEAT the oven to 350°F.

TO MAKE THE CAKE, sift together the flour, salt, baking powder, cinnamon, nutmeg, and allspice in a medium bowl.

IN A MEDIUM BOWL using a stand mixer on medium speed, beat 6 of the egg whites with the cream of tartar on high speed until light and fluffy. Gradually add the corn syrup and continue beating until stiff peaks form. Do not underbeat.

IN A LARGE BOWL, with clean beaters, beat the 7 egg yolks with the molasses and vanilla on high speed until thick. Use a spatula to blend in the flour mixture, and then gently fold in the beaten egg whites, followed by the chopped walnuts.

POUR the batter into an ungreased 10-inch Bundt or other tube-shaped pan and bake for 40 to 50 minutes, until a skewer or table knife inserted into the cake comes out clean. Remove the pan from the oven and immediately invert it onto a wire rack, leaving the cake in the pan to cool completely.

WHILE the cake cools, make the frosting. Using a stand mixer and clean beaters, beat the remaining egg white on medium speed until stiff, and then add the heavy cream and continue to beat until thick. Use a spatula to fold in the confectioners' sugar, cinnamon, and salt.

GENTLY remove the cooled cake from the pan. Using sewing thread or thin dental floss, cut the cake into three horizontal layers, and completely frost each layer as you stack them together. Smooth the frosting over the entire cake and decorate the cake with the walnut halves.

Old Henry has a friend up north he met years ago. Now every year this friend sends a huge package of used clothing for Henry and the poor folks of southern Appalachia. "I ain't got the heart to tell him it ain't like that here," Henry says. "You know how them northerners think," he added. "He's workin' his way to Heaven and I ain't gonna be the one who stops him. I just send them on to them poor folks out west."

MELUNGEON WEDDING CAKE

makes one sheet cake

THIS IS A MELUNGEON RECIPE found in a diary from the 1860s. The original read, "Take the whites of 14 eggs . . . 1 cup butter, beaten to a cream . . . 2 cups sugar . . . finely Sentamon. Mix 3 teaspoons of yeast powders with 3 cups flour. Mix all thoroughly, add flavoring to suit. Bake 1 hour." The original recipe says nothing about frosting the cake, so I've also included a frosting recipe, which follows.

---

1 cup (2 sticks) unsalted butter, at room temperature

2 cups firmly packed light brown sugar

2 teaspoons ground cinnamon (or more, if you like)

1 tablespoon vanilla extract

14 egg yolks

3 cups self-rising flour

1 tablespoon baking powder

1 ¼ cups half-and-half or whole milk

PREHEAT the oven to 350°F and lightly grease and flour a 9 by 13-inch baking dish.

USING a stand mixer, beat together the butter, brown sugar, cinnamon, and vanilla on medium speed until creamy. Add the egg yolks two or three at a time, beating after each addition. (There are just so many egg yolks that it's easier to add them a few at a time.) Slowly add the flour and baking powder, a little at a time, and beat until a thick batter forms. Add the half-and-half a little at a time, beating until smooth.

POUR the batter into the prepared pan and bake for 45 minutes to1 hour. Start checking after 35 minutes. The cake is done when a toothpick inserted into the center of the cake comes out clean. Let the cake cool in the pan on a wire rack before frosting it.

Wedding Cake Frosting

makes about 2 cups

Although this is not part of the original Melungeon recipe, it goes great with the cake, so I thought I would include it. It's a basic and very simple recipe. I like the flavor of vanilla, so I always add a bit more.

4 cups confectioners' sugar

¾ cup vegetable shortening

½ cup half-and-half

1 teaspoon almond extract

1 teaspoon vanilla extract

IN A MEDIUM BOWL using a stand mixer, beat the confectioners' sugar and shortening on medium speed until fluffy. Slowly beat in the half-and-half, almond extract, and vanilla. Spread the frosting over the cooled cake.

back in "the good old days," a woman would get up before dawn to do the family baking. She got out her large wooden bowl, put all of the ingredients in, and, using the homemade wooden spoon that her husband had carved, beat the ingredients until they became a batter. The warmth from her oven kept the family cabin warm as she went about her tasks. Sounds romantic, doesn't it? Well, it wasn't and isn't, as I found out when I tried it. These old-fashioned cakes are delicious, but it can be a lot of work beating the batters by hand. I've included stand mixer directions where appropriate.

The first time I tested the Melungeon Wedding Cake, using the original instructions, it came out looking like bread pudding, but it was delicious. After consulting with Barb Land, a trained pastry chef and owner of the Sweetest Touch, I learned that yeast isn't just yeast anymore. These days, professional bakers use cake yeast, and apparently it isn't readily available at the grocery store. Because of that, I've rewritten the recipe to make it easy for the modern baker. I've removed the yeast, added vanilla to the recipe, changed the sugar to brown sugar because the original translation, by a family member, called for brown sugar, and put a little more cinnamon in than would normally be called for and added self-rising flour. This cake is very good, and I found myself sneaking into the kitchen to get just one more tiny piece. You might want to consider that, because of the number of egg yolks, this is more of a special-occasion cake.

MOUNTAIN MOLASSES STACK CAKE

makes one 8-inch layer cake

THIS IS A TRADITIONAL MOUNTAIN FAVORITE. Each family would bring a single layer to a reunion or other celebration, and the layers would be assembled into a multilayered cake or several smaller cakes. The traditional filling is apple butter. I was at a meeting a while back when someone brought this as a single layer with the filling on the top. It was so good that we all asked for the recipe.

───────◆───────

CAKE

½ cup firmly packed brown sugar

8 tablespoons (1 stick) unsalted butter, at room temperature

1 large egg

½ cup molasses

½ cup buttermilk

1 teaspoon vanilla extract

¼ teaspoon ground nutmeg

2 cups all-purpose flour

1 tablespoon baking powder

¼ teaspoon baking soda

½ teaspoon salt

FILLING

2 cups finely chopped apples

½ cup water

1 cup firmly packed brown sugar

1 teaspoon ground cinnamon

PREHEAT the oven to 350°F. Lightly grease and flour the outside bottom of two 8-inch round cake pans.

TO MAKE THE CAKE, cream together the brown sugar and butter in a large bowl until light. Slowly add the egg and molasses and blend well. Beat in the buttermilk, vanilla, and nutmeg.

IN ANOTHER BOWL, sift together the flour, baking powder, baking soda, and salt.

SLOWLY add the flour mixture to the molasses mixture and mix until thoroughly incorporated.

POUR half of the batter into each prepared cake pan. Bake for 15 minutes, or until a toothpick inserted into the center of each cake comes out clean. Let the cakes cool on their pans on a wire rack.

WHILE the cakes are cooling, make the filling. In a medium saucepan over medium heat, combine the apples and water. Cook, stirring occasionally, until the apples are tender. Stir in the brown sugar and cinnamon. Bring to a boil and, stirring constantly, cook the mixture until a light syrup forms.

PLACE one of the cooled cake layers on a serving plate and spread half of the filling on top. Place the second layer on top, and spread the remaining filling over the top.

in the southern Appalachian region, cakes are usually four to six layers tall. Creating several thin layers is accomplished by baking two or three regular round cake layers, and then taking a sewing thread and, using it like a knife, drawing it toward you through the middle of the cooled cake layers. In this way, a two-layer cake recipe becomes a four-layer cake, and three cake layers become six. This allows for all manner of creativity, and many cakes have a variety of fillings separate from the frosting. There is something quite grand about a tall cake, and presenting it to your guests is sure to get a positive "Oooh."

BLUEBERRY POUND CAKE

makes one 9-inch loaf

WE ARE FORTUNATE TO HAVE BLUEBERRY FARMS in the mountains. Going as a family or just by yourself to pick blueberries and then coming home to create something out of them is quite a treat. Somehow your baking tastes better if you've picked the berries yourself.

---

1 cup (2 sticks) unsalted butter, at room temperature

3 cups sugar

1½ teaspoons vanilla extract

½ teaspoon freshly squeezed lemon juice

6 large eggs

3 cups all-purpose flour

¼ teaspoon baking soda

3 cups plus 1½ cups fresh or defrosted frozen blueberries

1 cup sour cream

Crystal Blue Blueberry Glaze, for serving (recipe follows)

GLAZE

½ cup fresh or defrosted frozen blueberries

1 cup sugar

2 tablespoons cornstarch

1 cup water

PREHEAT the oven to 350°F and lightly grease and flour a 9-inch loaf pan.

IN A LARGE BOWL, cream together the butter and sugar until light and fluffy. Beat in the vanilla and lemon juice. Add the eggs one at a time, beating after each addition. Sift the flour and baking soda into the butter mixture and blend well. Fold in 3 cups of the blueberries and the sour cream.

SPOON the batter into the prepared loaf pan and bake for about 1 hour, or until a toothpick inserted into the center of the cake comes out clean. Let the cake cool in the pan on a wire rack, and then gently invert the loaf onto a serving plate. Place the remaining 1½ cups blueberries on top of the pound cake, and then pour the glaze over the top.

TO MAKE THE GLAZE, crush the blueberries through a strainer. Reserve the juice and the crushed berries.

IN A MEDIUM SAUCEPAN over medium-low heat, combine the sugar, cornstarch, and water. Cook, stirring, until the sugar and cornstarch dissolve, and then add the crushed blueberries and their juice and cook until the mixture thickens and begins to bubble. Boil for 2 minutes, or until the mixture turns transparent, stirring constantly. Let the glaze cool completely before pouring it over the cake.

RAW APPLE CAKE

makes 1 Bundt cake

THIS IS AN EXCELLENT RECIPE from the Walnut Lane Inn in Lyman, South Carolina. Nestled under a canopy of majestic walnut trees, the inn and grounds are what's left of an old cotton plantation. Located in Spartanburg County, Lyman sits in the foothills of the Blue Ridge Mountains. Enjoy Cowpens National Battlefield, where General Daniel Morgan's troops defeated the British during the Revolutionary War, or visit the many cultural activities in the area. This recipe came from the owner's mother, and he wanted me to know that "it is the best cake to serve guests."

CAKE

2 cups granulated sugar

1½ cups vegetable oil

3 large eggs

1 teaspoon vanilla extract

3 cups all-purpose flour

½ teaspoon salt

1 teaspoon baking soda

3 cups peeled and chopped tart apples, such as Granny Smith

1½ cups chopped pecans or walnuts

TOPPING

1 cup light brown sugar

1½ sticks margarine

¼ cup milk

PREHEAT the oven to 350°F and lightly grease or spray a 10-inch Bundt pan.

IN A LARGE BOWL using a stand mixer, beat together the sugar, oil, eggs, and vanilla until well blended.

IN A MEDIUM BOWL, whisk together the flour, salt, and baking soda, and then stir them into the sugar mixture. Use a spatula to fold in the apples and nuts.

POUR the batter into the prepared pan and bake for 1 hour and 10 minutes, or until a skewer or table knife inserted into the cake comes out clean. Allow the cake to cool a little on a wire rack while you make the topping.

COMBINE the brown sugar, margarine, and milk in a medium saucepan and bringing it to rolling boil over medium-low heat. Cook, stirring occasionally, for about 3 minutes, or until the sugar is completely dissolved. Pour the topping over the warm cake and serve immediately.

CORNMEAL COFFEE CAKE

serves 10 to 12

CORNMEAL MAY SEEM LIKE AN ODD CHOICE for coffee cake, but in the mountains cornmeal is widely used in baking. I like this coffee cake because it's basic. You can use almost any kind of fruit with it, or no fruit at all.

CAKE

1½ cups yellow cornmeal

½ cup all-purpose flour

½ cup sugar

4 tablespoons (½ stick) unsalted butter, at room temperature

1 large egg, beaten

½ cup buttermilk

1 (8-ounce) package cream cheese, at room temperature

TOPPING

1 cup thinly sliced fresh strawberries

½ cup slivered almonds

1 cup fresh or defrosted frozen blueberries

⅓ cup sugar

2 tablespoons melted unsalted butter

PREHEAT the oven to 375°F. Lightly grease and flour a 9 by 13-inch baking dish.

IN A LARGE BOWL, combine the cornmeal, flour, sugar, and butter. Blend well until the mixture is the consistency of crumbs.

IN ANOTHER BOWL, mix together the egg, buttermilk, and cream cheese. Slowly add the egg mixture to the flour mixture and stir until blended. Spread the batter evenly into the prepared pan.

FOR THE TOPPING, arrange the strawberries over the top of the batter.

SPRINKLE on the slivered almonds, followed by the blueberries. Sprinkle the sugar over the top, and then drizzle on the melted butter.

BAKE for 40 to 50 minutes, until the edges of the cake are golden brown and a toothpick inserted in the center of the cake comes out clean. Let cool on a wire rack.

PIECRUST DOUGH

makes one 9-inch double crust

THIS PIECRUST RECIPE, WHICH dates back to the late 1940s, is very good. The first time I tasted it was at a Thanksgiving dinner, and the hostess was a little upset that I found this crust more interesting than the pie filling. She seemed to be happier when I asked for both recipes. I would use this with almost any pie recipe, especially sweet potato, pumpkin, squash, or other vegetable pies. Cut the recipe in half for a single crust.

---

2 cups sifted all-purpose flour

1 tablespoon sugar

1 teaspoon salt

¾ cup vegetable shortening

1 egg yolk

1 tablespoon freshly squeezed lemon juice

¼ cup milk

1 egg white (if baking the shell)

IN A LARGE BOWL, sift together the flour, sugar, and salt. Use a fork to cut in the shortening until it is thoroughly and evenly incorporated.

IN A SMALL BOWL, mix together the egg yolk, lemon juice, and milk. Gently fold the egg yolk mixture into the flour mixture to form a soft dough. Turn the dough out onto a floured surface, cover it with a bowl, and let it rest for 10 minutes.

PAT the dough into a ball, divide it in half, and shape each half into a flattened disk. Use the dough as directed in a pie recipe.

IF YOU WANT TO make a baked pie shell, preheat the oven to 450°F. Roll out one of the dough disks until it is about 1 inch wider than the outside rim of your pie pan. Transfer the dough to the pie pan, flute the edges, and brush the crust with beaten egg white. Prick the bottom lightly and bake the shell for 8 to 10 minutes, until golden brown.

SOUTHERN BLACKBERRY COBBLER

serves 6 to 8

IN SOUTHERN APPALACHIA, everyone has a favorite blackberry cobbler recipe. And everywhere one goes, one is invited to taste "the best cobbler in the South!" This recipe would go well with a half recipe of the Piecrust Dough (page 147).

———— ◆ ————

5 cups fresh or defrosted frozen blackberries

¾ cup plus 1 tablespoon sugar

1 tablespoon cornstarch

⅛ teaspoon salt

1 tablespoon unsalted butter, cut into bits

Pastry for 9-inch single-crust pie (page 147)

1 tablespoon milk

PREHEAT the oven to 425°F.

WASH and dry the blackberries if necessary and pour them into a 9-inch square baking dish.

SIFT together the ¾ cup sugar, the cornstarch, and salt into a bowl, then sprinkle the mixture over the blackberries. Dot with the butter.

ROLL OUT the pie pastry on a lightly floured surface into a 9-inch square, and then place the pastry on top of the blackberries; trim the edges and seal them against the dish. Make several slits in the top of the crust to allow steam to escape. Brush the pastry top with the milk and sprinkle with the remaining 1 tablespoon sugar.

BAKE for 30 minutes, or until the crust is golden brown and the filling is bubbly. Let cool on a wire rack.

BUTTERMILK PIE

makes one 9-inch pie

THE GREYSTONE INN, in Lake Toxaway, North Carolina, is an award-winning 1915 six-level Swiss-style mansion, luxuriously furnished with period furniture and reproductions. High tea on the sun porch and a champagne cruise on the twenty-six-passenger mahogany launch Miss Lucy reflect the lifestyle so closely identified with the likes of Thomas Edison, Harvey Firestone, Henry Ford, and others who discovered that there is no more beautiful location than the Greystone Inn. Their version of the traditional southern sweet pie is delicious.

GRAHAM CRACKER CRUST

1⅓ cups graham cracker crumbs

⅔ cup granulated sugar

1 cup (2 sticks) unsalted butter

¼ cup finely chopped pecans

FILLING

2 (8-ounce) packages cream cheese or Neufchâtel, at room temperature

3 cups granulated sugar

2 teaspoons vanilla extract

1 cup sour cream

2 cups buttermilk

½ cup heavy whipping cream

8 large eggs

BROWN SUGAR SAUCE

1½ cups firmly packed brown sugar

1 teaspoon vanilla extract

½ cup heavy whipping cream

⅓ cup sour cream

PREHEAT the oven to 350°F and grease a 9-inch springform pan.

TO MAKE THE CRUST, combine the graham cracker crumbs, sugar, butter, and pecans in a large bowl and mix until all of the crumbs are moistened. Press the mixture firmly into the pan and bake for 7 minutes, or until golden brown. Let the crust cool completely on a wire rack.

TO MAKE THE FILLING, mix the cream cheese, sugar, vanilla, sour cream, buttermilk, and heavy whipping cream until smooth. Add the eggs one at a time, mixing well after each addition. Pour the filling into the crust and bake for about 1 hour, or until the filling is set. Let the pie cool on a wire rack.

TO MAKE THE SAUCE, combine the brown sugar, vanilla, heavy whipping cream, and sour cream in a large bowl and stir until smooth.

CUT the cooled pie into wedges and drizzle the sauce over each slice before serving.

SHAKER LEMON PIE

Makes one 9-inch pie

THE SHAKER TAVERN, BUILT in 1869 as a business venture for the South Union Shakers, housed a hotel for the "people of the world." The Shakers leased the building to an outside interest for one hundred dollars a month, leaving its management to the "world." Today the Shaker Tavern is owned and operated by the Shaker Museum at South Union, Kentucky. This recipe has a delicate taste and isn't as overwhelming as some lemon pies can be.

1 lemon, sliced paper thin

1 cup plus ½ cup sugar

Pastry for 9-inch single-crust pie (page 147)

4 large eggs

¾ cup evaporated milk

⅓ cup unsalted butter, melted

1 tablespoon all-purpose flour

1 tablespoon cornmeal (or an additional
    2 tablespoons flour)

PREHEAT the oven to 350°F.

PLACE the lemon slices in a medium bowl with 1 cup of the sugar and let it stand for about an hour. Roll out the pie pastry and place it in a 9-inch pie pan.

IN A LARGE BOWL, combine the eggs, evaporated milk, and butter and beat well. In a separate bowl, mix together the flour, cornmeal, and the remaining ½ cup sugar. Add the flour mixture to the egg mixture and blend well.

REMOVE the lemon slices from the sugar and stir the sugar from the bowl into the egg mixture. Pour the filling into the unbaked pie shells and arrange the lemon slices over the top.

BAKE for 45 minutes, or until the top of the pie is lightly browned. Be careful not to overbake. Let cool on a wire rack.

GEORGE WASHINGTON CARVER'S SWEET POTATO PIE

makes one 9-inch pie

AS DIRECTOR OF THE EXPERIMENT STATION at the Tuskegee Institute, in Alabama, George Washington Carver's work with sweet potatoes changed the agricultural economy of the South and southern Appalachian region. He issued bulletins to farmers advising on the latest methods for planting and using their crops. Everything the farmer needed to know was in the bulletin. And, as he was a talented and innovative cook, he always added a few recipes. This recipe is from Bulletin no. 38, November 1936. The "trick" to this pie is not to overcook the potatoes, because they have to absorb a lot of liquid. It comes out of the oven looking lumpy and marbled, but it's so delicious that you won't mind. In translating this recipe for the modern kitchen, I tried to make it as simple as possible.

---

2 very large, fat yellow sweet potatoes

Pastry for 9-inch double-crust pie (page 147)

⅛ teaspoon ground nutmeg

⅛ teaspoon ground allspice

¼ teaspoon ground cloves

⅛ teaspoon ground ginger

2 tablespoons unsalted butter

½ pint heavy whipping cream

¾ cup sugar

¼ cup hot water

6 tablespoons molasses

1 tablespoon all-purpose flour

PLACE the unpeeled sweet potatoes in a large pot and cover them with water. Turn the heat to medium-low and bring to a low boil. Cover and cook for about 40 minutes, or until a fork pierces the flesh with resistance. You want an almost-done potato. Let the potatoes cool, and drain off the water. Peel the potatoes and slice them lengthwise ⅛ to ¼ inch thick. Put the slices on a plate and set aside.

PLACE an oven rack in the center of the oven and preheat the oven to 350°F. Roll out one disk of the pie pastry and line the bottom of a 9 by 2-inch pie pan or a 9-inch square baking dish with the dough. Do not prick the dough. Arrange the potato slices to completely cover the bottom crust, and continue layering to a depth of 2 inches.

EVENLY sprinkle the top of the potatoes with the nutmeg, allspice, cloves, and ginger. Cut the butter into six or eight pieces and dot them around the top of the potatoes.

IN A LARGE MEASURING CUP, combine the cream, sugar, hot water, and molasses. Stir to blend well, then evenly pour the mixture over the potatoes. Sprinkle the top of the pie with the flour.

ROLL out the remaining disk of pie pastry, place it over the pie filling, and crimp the edges to seal. Make a slit or two in the top crust. Place a baking sheet on the middle rack of the oven and place the pie in the center of the sheet. Bake for 40 to 45 minutes, until the crust is nicely browned and the pie is bubbling. Let cool a bit on a wire rack, and serve hot.

"granny women"

Granny women, sometimes called *granny witches*, are a tradition that still exists in the mountains. They are midwives and healers. The knowledge of old healing methods came over from northern Europe as early as the 1500s. Granny women pass their knowledge on to their daughters, who in turn pass it on to their daughters. It is rare to have the craft passed outside of the family.

Folks still seek out granny women for help now and then. They can trust that the granny will give them good advice, and these encounters are usually treated in confidence. If they need to go to a doctor or to the hospital, she'll let them know.

These two remedies were taught to me by a local granny woman.

TO STOP a persistent cough, rub the bottoms of your feet with Vicks VapoRub. As strange as it sounds, it works.

TO STOP the bleeding in a bad cut so that you can get to the doctor's office or hospital, gather a handful of cobwebs and place them over the cut. Then wrap tightly with a bandage or cloth. The bleeding will stop. Since a cobweb is made from spider silk and is sticky and strong, this makes perfect sense. However, webs are usually full of dust, so the doctor's visit is important.

BUTTER TARTS

makes 24 tarts

AN OLD APPALACHIAN FAVORITE, butter tarts are considered to be more Canadian than southern, but somehow they made it down south. Similar traditional Scottish treats are called Ecclefechan butter tarts, and I suspect they traveled to the New World long ago, where the dish was adopted by southern mountain folk. Scottish descendants of those early settlers to the region keep their traditions alive in annual Scottish games, music, dancing, and museums. While I was exploring local Scottish culture for this recipe, I met with a gentleman in an outdoor restaurant in Gatlinburg, Tennessee. "You should go talk to James," he said while giving me directions to find him. "He's up thar on that mountain all by hisself and I hear he's lookin' for a wife," he added with a laugh. He then told me that James was a descendant of early settlers and that he had a long beard and was often seen walking through the forest wearing a kilt. "How do you feel about a man wearin' a dress?" he asked. "Does he have nice knees?" I inquired. We both laughed and drank our sweet tea.

Cornmeal, for dusting

2 large eggs

½ cup light corn syrup

3 tablespoons unsalted butter, melted

1 ¼ cups firmly packed brown sugar

1 cup raisins

¼ cup finely chopped walnuts or pecans

2 teaspoons white vinegar

½ teaspoon vanilla extract

Pinch of salt

Pastry for 2 (9-inch) double-crust pies (page 147)

PREHEAT the oven to 350°F. Lightly grease two 12-cup muffin pans, dust them with cornmeal, and shake out any excess.

IN A LARGE BOWL, beat the eggs until frothy. Beat in the corn syrup, melted butter, and brown sugar. Stir in the raisins, nuts, vinegar, vanilla, and salt.

ROLL OUT one pie pastry disk on a floured surface to ⅛ inch thick and cut out as many 4-inch circles as you can, rerolling the scraps if necessary. Repeat with the remaining pastry disks until you have twenty-four 4-inch circles. (You may not use the fourth pastry disk. If not, you can wrap it tightly and refrigerate or freeze it and save it for a single-crust pie.) Press each circle into one of the prepared muffin cups. The dough in the cups should be about ⅛ inch thick when you're finished pressing it in.

FILL each dough cup two-thirds full with filling. Bake for 15 to 20 minutes, until the edges of the crusts are golden brown. Let cool on a wire rack.

BAKEWELL TART

makes one 9-inch tart

THE BRAESIDE INN in Sevierville, Tennessee, is a quiet and cozy Scottish-themed inn just a few minutes' drive from the Great Smoky Mountains National Park, and the views are incredible. This traditional British tart makes a lovely treat with tea. Tradition holds that the tart was created by accident in Derbyshire, England, in 1820, when the cook at an inn added eggs and almonds to a jelly tart. It was a great success and still is to this day.

Pastry for 9-inch single-crust pie (page 147)

2 tablespoons lemon curd

2 tablespoons strawberry jam

4 tablespoons (½ stick) unsalted butter

6 tablespoons superfine sugar

Grated zest and juice of ½ lemon

1 large egg

4 heaping tablespoons cake crumbs (can use crumbled ladyfingers)

4 ounces almonds, ground (8 tablespoons)

PREHEAT the oven to 375°F. Lightly grease a 9-inch removable-bottom tart pan.

ROLL out the pie pastry about ⅛ inch thick and a little larger than the tart pan. Place the rolling pin in the center and fold the pastry over it. Then transfer it to the tart pan, laying it down evenly and carefully. Using your hands, carefully press the pastry around the sides and bottom of the pan. Spread pastry with lemon curd and then jam.

IN A LARGE BOWL, cream the butter until it is soft and fluffy. Add the sugar and lemon zest and beat until the mixture is light and well blended.

IN A SMALL BOWL, lightly beat the egg, and then add it a little at a time to the butter mixture, stirring constantly. Stir in the lemon juice, cake crumbs, and almonds. Spread the mixture on top of the jam.

BAKE the tart for 35 to 45 minutes, until set and golden brown. Let cool completely on a wire rack before serving.

APPLE FRITTERS

makes 8

APPLE FRITTERS ARE A little like mini apple pies, and they're delicious. There are so many ways to serve them. They can be rolled in cinnamon and granulated sugar as they are here, dusted with confectioners' sugar, served alongside vanilla ice cream, or drizzled with a warm caramel sauce (recipe follows). Restaurants around these parts very often serve a basket of apple fritters as an appetizer. They are delicious broken open and buttered.

Vegetable oil, for frying

1 cup all-purpose flour

2 tablespoons plus ½ cup sugar

1 large egg

¾ cup milk

1 Granny Smith apple, peeled, cored, and cut into
    8 slices

1 tablespoon ground cinnamon

CARAMEL SAUCE

1½ cups sugar

½ cup boiling water

FILL a deep skillet three-quarters full with vegetable oil, and heat the oil to 370°F on an instant-read thermometer. You can also use a deep fryer.

IN A MEDIUM BOWL, combine the flour, 2 tablespoons of the sugar, the egg, and milk and blend well. Drop the apple slices into the batter and coat them well. Deep-fry the battered slices, in small batches, for 6 to 7 minutes, until golden brown. Do not overcrowd the fryer or skillet. Transfer the fritters to paper towels to drain.

MIX the remaining ½ cup of sugar and the cinnamon together in a shallow dish. Roll the warm fritters in the cinnamon sugar and serve.

TO MAKE THE SAUCE: In a heavy, dry saucepan over medium-low heat, carefully melt the sugar. Stir constantly so the sugar doesn't burn. When the sugar turns a golden brown, slowly and very carefully add the boiling water. Still stirring, blend well and cook for about 3 minutes. Serve warm.

OLD-FASHIONED INDIAN PUDDING WITH CINNAMON WHIPPED CREAM

serves 6

INDIAN PUDDING IS AN OLD AND BELOVED American recipe. The recipe is found in books as early as 1822, and the name most likely comes from the "Indian meal" or cornmeal used. The native Cherokee make a similar pudding without the spices, and use sorghum molasses. From what I've learned, this pudding seems to have been created at Plymouth Colony in the late 1620s, when dairy cattle were brought over from England and milk products became available to the colonists. Serve it warm.

PUDDING

4 cups milk

¼ cup yellow cornmeal

2 tablespoons unsalted butter, at room temperature

½ cup molasses

¼ cup sugar

½ teaspoon ground cinnamon

½ teaspoon ground ginger

½ teaspoon salt

CINNAMON WHIPPED CREAM

1 cup heavy whipping cream

1 cup sugar

½ teaspoon ground cinnamon

PREHEAT the oven to 250°F.

IN A LARGE SAUCEPAN over low heat, scald 2 cups of the milk.

IN A SMALL BOWL, combine the cornmeal and ½ cup of the remaining milk. Pour the mixture into the scalded milk and cook, stirring, for 10 minutes.

REMOVE the pan from the heat and stir in the butter and molasses. Add the sugar, cinnamon, ginger, and salt and blend well. Stir in the remaining 1½ cups milk.

POUR the pudding into a 1½-quart casserole dish and bake for 3 hours. The top should look like the top of a coffee cake.

WHILE the pudding is baking, make the whipped cream. In a medium bowl using a stand mixer, beat the cream on medium speed until soft peaks form. Add the sugar and cinnamon and continue to beat until stiff peaks form. Serve the pudding with a dollop of whipped cream.

southern appalachian dictionary

These are a few examples of words and phases in the southern Appalachian language. The southern Appalachian dialect is an academically recognized language and has been cataloged and placed in dictionaries, a fact that is proudly pointed out when the language is laughed at by outsiders.

A

a back of—behind, out back: "They was a back of the house."

a coon's age—a long time

afeared—afraid, scared

afixin'—getting ready to do something

agin—against something

aim—planning or intending: "I aim to cut the wood."

B

blowed—blew: "That wind blowed them trees down."

book read—well educated

borned—born: "He was borned in Kentuck."

C

catched—caught: "He'd kill that bar if he ever catched him."

choicey—choosy, particular

come hell or high water—in spite of

comes a tide—a big flood is coming

crick—a "kink" in your neck or back

crick—a small stream

D

dawg—dog: "That dawg was done eat up when that bar got hold of 'im."

directly—soon, in a little while

doin's—an event

drug—dragged: "He drug him down to the crick."

E

eat up—badly hurt: "That dawg was done eat up when that bar got hold of 'im."

F

fatmeat or fatback—bacon

feller—fellow, man: "She ain't got no feller."

fetch—to get or bring: "Fetch me that saw, son."

fish pole—fishing rod

folks—people: "Folks around these parts . . ."

fur piece—a long way to go

G

git er done—finish something

give in—give up: "I ain't give in yet."

granny woman—midwife

granny woman—mountain witch, potion maker

gullywasher—torrential rain

H

hear tell—heard of: "I hear tell of that."

het up—agitated

hisself—himself: "He done rest hisself."

hit the shucks—go to bed on a
   corn husk mattress

I

iffin—if: "Iffin you folks want . . ."

in a family way—pregnant

J

job—jab, strike

K

knowed—knew: "I knowed him as a youngin'."

L

lay out—camping under the stars

leave out—to leave

listen at—listen to

lit out—left: "He just lit out."

lollygaggin'—fooling around; being lazy

M

mess of—a whole lot or bunch

N

nigh way—shortcut

no count—no good

O

oldsters—oldtimers

outen—out of something

P

parts—a place: "You from these parts?"

passel—an indefinite number of
   people, animals, or things

peaked—feeling ill

plot—a piece of land: "Got a nice plot of land."

plum—completely: "I am plum tuckered out!"

put out—angry

R

rattle trap—noisemaking device

S

shed of—get rid of

skittish—nervous, anxious

smackdab—right in the middle of something

sour milk—buttermilk

sweet milk—fresh milk

T

take a gander—to look at; to
   check something out

take up—to arrest

take up—support: "He'll take up fer ya."

throwed—threw: "They throwed
   them in the hole."

tuckered—tired, worn out

W

ways—distance: "Just a ways up the hill . . ."

we'ums—us and our kin

Y

y'all have a Blessed day—what you
   say when leaving a person

yes, ma'am; yes, sir—manners
   are always expected

yet—still: "They's livin' there yet."

youngin'—child

you'ums—you and your kin

SE-LU I-SA U-GA-NA-S-DA (CORNMEAL COOKIES)

makes 1½ dozen

THIS CHEROKEE RECIPE MAKES LUMPY, round cookies that are really good, and by the 1820s it found its way into a cookbook. The Cherokee were farmers and cattle ranchers here in the mountains, and by 1835 they were outproducing their European counterparts in the region. Milk and milk products entered the culture and as a result many Cherokee recipes seem similar to European recipes, although it's hard to decipher which came first.

12 tablespoons (¾ cup) unsalted butter or margarine

¾ cup sugar

1 large egg

1 teaspoon vanilla extract

1½ cups all-purpose flour

½ cup cornmeal

1 teaspoon baking powder

¼ teaspoon salt

½ cup raisins (optional)

PREHEAT the oven to 350°F and grease a baking sheet.

IN A LARGE BOWL, cream together the butter and sugar. Add the egg and vanilla and beat until smooth. Stir in the flour, cornmeal, baking powder, salt, and raisins, mixing well.

DROP the dough by rounded tablespoons onto the prepared baking sheet. Bake for about 15 minutes, or until the cookies are lightly browned. Let the cookies cool on a wire rack.

living in the southern Appalachian Mountains is living closely with nature, and childhood memories are filled with stories about accompanying Maw-Maw or Paw-Paw into the woods to gather wild berries, nuts, and other edibles and tales of lazy days spent fishin' for dinner or just exploring and bringing back wildflowers for Mother. I love to hear these stories because tellers of such tales get a distant look in their eyes and a warm smile comes over their face. It's the sharing of experience and the opportunity to spend time learning from loved ones that's so special here. What may be taken for granted in this ancient place isn't found much anymore in other places. It doesn't matter what the subject is, there's always a story to go with it.

CHERRY-BERRY BLONDIES
makes 2 dozen

THE BUCKHORN INN HAS been a favorite destination in Gatlinburg, Tennessee, since 1938. It's surrounded by a beautiful pine and hemlock forest, and it has a great view of the Great Smoky Mountains. Their blondies can be baked ahead and cooled completely (but not cut into squares), and then wrapped tightly with plastic wrap and kept at room temperature until ready to cut and serve. These are a popular treat at the inn.

1 cup dried cranberries

1 cup dried tart cherries

1 cup golden raisins

1 cup boiling water

2½ cups all-purpose flour

1½ teaspoons baking soda

1 teaspoon salt

¼ teaspoon ground cinnamon

1 cup (2 sticks) unsalted butter, melted and cooled

2 cups sugar

3 large eggs

1½ teaspoons vanilla extract

1 cup whole skin-on almonds, toasted and coarsely chopped

8 ounces bittersweet chocolate, coarsely chopped

PREHEAT the oven to 400°F. Butter and lightly flour a 12 by 17-inch baking pan. Place the cranberries, cherries, and raisins in a small bowl and pour the boiling water over them. Let soak for 20 minutes, and then drain the fruit well in a colander.

IN A MEDIUM BOWL, stir together the flour, baking soda, salt, and cinnamon.

IN A LARGE BOWL using a stand mixer, beat together the melted butter, sugar, eggs, and vanilla on high speed until creamy, about 1 minute. Turn the speed to low, add the flour mixture, and mix until just combined. Use a spatula to stir in the fruit, almonds, and chocolate.

SPREAD the batter evenly in the prepared pan and bake for 25 to 30 minutes, until golden brown and a toothpick or skewer inserted in the center comes out clean. Let cool completely in the pan on a wire rack. Run a thin knife around the edges of the pan to loosen the blondies, and then cut them into roughly 3-inch squares.

PEPPERKAKOR (SWEDISH GINGER COOKIES)

makes about 6 dozen

THE FIDDLERS GLEN BED AND BREAKFAST is a restored 1854 Carpenter Gothic home listed on the Jonesborough, Tennessee, Historic Registry. It is within walking distance of the shops on Main Street and the International Storytelling Center. The inn prides itself on its unique music room, where you can enjoy an assortment of musical instruments. These cookies they shared with me are very crisp and delicious. Since there are no eggs in the recipe, the chilled dough will keep for weeks in the refrigerator.

1 cup sugar

⅓ cup molasses

Scant ½ cup water

1 to 2 teaspoons ground ginger

2 teaspoons ground cinnamon

2 teaspoons ground cloves

1 tablespoon baking soda

1 cup (2 sticks) unsalted butter

4 cups all-purpose flour

IN A LARGE HEAVY SAUCEPAN over medium heat, bring the sugar, molasses, water, ginger, cinnamon, and cloves just to a boil. Remove the pan from the heat and add the baking soda. The mixture will foam up.

PLACE the butter in a large bowl and pour the hot mixture over it. Stir until the butter is completely melted. Add the flour a little at a time, stirring after each addition. Let the dough cool completely, and then cover the bowl and place it in the refrigerator overnight.

PREHEAT the oven to 350°F. Knead the dough thoroughly on a floured surface. Roll out the dough to about a ⅛-inch thickness. Cut out shapes as desired and place them on ungreased baking sheets. Bake the cookies for 7 to 10 minutes, until golden brown. Use a metal spatula to remove the cookies from the baking sheets to cool on wire racks.

these cookies bring back memories for the Fiddlers Glen innkeeper: "We spent a year in Sweden when I was just a baby. My dad, Dr. Arthur Waltner, was a nuclear physicist at North Carolina State University who went to the University of Stockholm as an exchange professor for the Atoms for Peace program in 1952. My mom brought the recipe back with us. We baked these at Christmastime with a bit of string under the dough. We would cut out mostly stars and bells and hang them as edible ornaments on our Christmas tree. Not surprisingly, we would have to rebake every day or so since they would all mysteriously disappear!"

SWEET TATER COOKIES

makes about 3 dozen

THIS IS A MELUNGEON RECIPE. Since the sweet potato is a vegetable, these could be called Vegetable Cookies. This lovely, old-fashioned cookie is the perfect treat. Serve them with a scoop of ice cream or just keep them in the cookie jar for those little hands to find.

1½ cups mashed cooked sweet potatoes

⅔ cup unsalted butter, melted

2 teaspoons grated orange zest

1 teaspoon freshly squeezed lemon juice

½ cup firmly packed brown sugar

½ cup dark molasses

1¾ cups all-purpose flour

½ teaspoon salt

½ teaspoon baking soda

1 teaspoon ground cinnamon

¼ teaspoon ground cloves

½ cup chopped walnuts or pecans

IN A LARGE BOWL, mix the potatoes and butter. Stir in the orange zest, lemon juice, brown sugar, and molasses.

IN A MEDIUM BOWL, sift together the flour, salt, baking soda, cinnamon, and cloves. Gradually stir them into the potato mixture, mixing well. Fold in the nuts. Refrigerate the batter for several hours before baking.

PREHEAT the oven to 350°F. Drop the batter by spoonfuls onto ungreased baking sheets and bake for 10 to 12 minutes, until dark golden brown. Transfer the cookies to a wire rack to cool.

Now old John had his eye on Miss Betty, an old maid, for the longest time, but he was shy. Every Sunday at church he would sit behind her and try to get up the courage to say something. One night, after a little liquid persuasion, he decided to call her up.

"Hello?" Miss Betty answered. John was so nervous that he blurted out, "Will you marry me?" Without hesitation, Miss Betty answered, "Sure! Who is this?"

SHORTBREAD

makes about 3 dozen

APPLEWOOD MANOR IS AN INN located in the Montford Historic District of Asheville, North Carolina. It's a New England–style home built by Captain James Adams Perry, and guests can see the original house plans and photos. Asheville is often called "the Paris of the South." Captain Perry fell in love with it, and visitors usually do, too. The innkeeper's own family can be traced back to the 1700s in North Carolina, but this is an authentic Scottish recipe from her late husband's family, who came to the U.S. from Scotland.

---

2 cups (4 sticks) unsalted butter, at room temperature

1¼ cups superfine sugar

6 cups sifted all-purpose flour

PREHEAT the oven to 350°F and line baking sheets with parchment paper.

BEAT the butter in a stand mixer on medium speed until fluffy, about 3 minutes.

GRADUALLY add the sugar, 1 tablespoon at a time, over the next hour, beating well between additions.

AFTER the hour of constant beating, turn the mixer speed to low and add the flour, mixing well.

LIGHTLY flour a large work surface and dump the dough into the center. Divide the dough into two equal portions and shape each portion into a 4-inch-thick roll about 6 inches long. At this point, you can wrap the dough in plastic wrap and refrigerate it for a few hours or overnight, until you're ready to use it.

CUT each roll into ¾-inch-thick slices. There should be eight or nine slices per roll. Divide each ¾-inch slice into three wedges. Place the cookies about 2 inches apart on the prepared baking sheets, and then pierce the tops of the cookies with a fork at least three times each.

BAKE the shortbread for about 20 minutes, or until golden. Let the cookies cool on a wire rack.

RICH COFFEE BROWNIES

makes 16

THE AZALEA INN in Banner Elk, North Carolina, has a great view of Horse Bottom Ridge. It's an award-winning bed-and-breakfast with cottages and a picket fence along the brick sidewalks of the town. Be sure to visit Karen's tearoom for an afternoon of "dress-up" fun. These brownies the inn shared with me are rich and gooey and perfect with tea or coffee.

4 ounces unsweetened chocolate

1 cup (2 sticks) unsalted butter

2 cups sugar

1 cup all-purpose flour

4 large eggs, beaten

2 teaspoons coffee liqueur

1 teaspoon instant coffee granules

1 cup semisweet chocolate chips

1 cup chopped walnuts or pecans (optional)

PREHEAT the oven to 325°F and grease a 9 by 13-inch baking dish.

IN A SMALL SAUCEPAN over low heat, melt the chocolate and butter, stirring constantly. Remove the pan from the heat.

IN A LARGE BOWL, combine the sugar and flour. Add the chocolate mixture, eggs, coffee liqueur, and coffee granules and stir until well blended. Fold in the chocolate chips and nuts.

SPREAD the batter into the prepared pan and bake for 35 minutes, or until the edges are firm. The center will be soft. Let the brownies cool for 30 minutes to 1 hour on a wire rack, and then refrigerate them for at least 2 hours before cutting them into 16 squares.

ORANGE FLOWER TEA CAKES

makes about 48

TEA CAKES COME IN a variety of styles. Some are flat cookies, some are miniature cupcakes, and some are tiny little cakes decorated for the occasion. They're delightful and perfect to serve with a cup of tea or coffee. Whether you are having an elaborate tea party using your best finery or just spending a cozy afternoon with a few friends, tea cakes are the perfect treat. This recipe makes tiny, delicious cakes. When the dish comes out of the oven there's an eggy aroma, but it soon disappears, and the combination of coriander and orange is lovely. You can ice and decorate them as you wish. I've included a frosting that I think you'll enjoy.

TEA CAKES

3 cups cake flour

1 tablespoon baking powder

½ teaspoon salt

1 cup (2 sticks) unsalted butter, at room temperature

2 cups granulated sugar

5 large eggs, at room temperature

1 tablespoon grated orange zest

½ tablespoon ground coriander

½ cup half-and-half

¼ cup orange juice

1 teaspoon vanilla extract

ICING

3 cups confectioners' sugar

1 teaspoon vanilla extract

6 tablespoons half-and-half

PREHEAT the oven to 350°F and lightly grease a 9 by 13-inch baking dish. Line the dish with parchment paper, leaving enough hanging over the sides so that you can use it to lift the cake from the pan. Once in place, lightly grease and flour the parchment paper. Set aside.

TO MAKE THE CAKES, sift together the flour, baking powder, and salt in a medium bowl.

IN A LARGE BOWL, combine the butter and sugar and cream until fluffy. Add the eggs, one at a time, beating after each addition. Beat in the orange zest and coriander. In a small bowl, stir together the half-and-half, orange juice, and vanilla. Slowly stir the half-and-half mixture into the butter mixture, mixing well. Slowly add the flour mixture and stir until well blended.

POUR the batter into the prepared baking dish and bake for 40 to 45 minutes, until a toothpick inserted in the center of the cake comes out clean. Let cool on a wire rack. When the cake is cooled, use the overhanging parchment paper to lift it from the pan. Place it on a cutting surface and cut it into 1½-inch squares.

TO MAKE THE ICING, combine the confectioners' sugar, vanilla, and half-and-half in a medium bowl and blend well. You want the consistency of a thick glaze that will drip down the sides of the cakes. Add more confectioners' sugar if it's too thin, or more half-and-half if it's too thick.

DRIZZLE a little icing over each cake and allow it to run down the sides. Let it set for a few minutes before serving.

OLD-FASHIONED SOUTHERN TEA CAKES

makes about 4 dozen

THE HAWKESDENE HOUSE IS located in the North Carolina mountains in Andrews, North Carolina. You can hike to a hidden waterfall, take a llama trek to a mountaintop, or pan for gold in the sparkling stream that meanders through the property. This is their old family recipe for a classic southern treat. If you want, you can use a cookie stamp dipped in a cinnamon-sugar mixture to stamp a design on top of each tea cake.

1 cup (2 sticks) unsalted butter, at room temperature

1 cup sugar, plus ⅔ cup for rolling the cakes

2 large eggs, beaten

1 teaspoon ground nutmeg

3½ cups all-purpose flour

2 tablespoons ground cinnamon

IN A LARGE BOWL, cream together the butter and 1 cup of the sugar. Add the eggs, nutmeg, and flour and mix well. Refrigerate the dough for 3 hours.

PREHEAT the oven to 350°F.

MIX the remaining ⅔ cup sugar with the cinnamon in a bowl. Form the dough into balls the size of a quarter and roll the balls in the cinnamon sugar. Place on ungreased baking sheets and bake for 8 to 10 minutes, until the edges start to turn golden brown. Transfer the tea cakes to a wire rack to cool.

what is a tea cake?

Simply put, a tea cake is a soft cookie. Tea cakes vary in size, shape, and appearance. They can be decorated, covered in icing like a tiny cake, or treated in any manner of creative ways. When a proper southern lady serves tea, she also serves tea cakes. It's a lovely old southern tradition that survives to this day.

chapter 9

BEVERAGES

BREAKFAST PUNCH

makes 1 gallon

THIS RECIPE IS FROM THE COLUMBUS STREET INN in Fayette, Alabama. The original house was built in 1870 by John Buford Sanford and his wife, Margaret Susan Robertson. Mr. Sanford, who was known as "Colonel Sanford" even though he was only a private in Company B of the 10th Alabama Infantry, saw action at Bull Run, Gettysburg, Antietam, and other major battles of the Civil War. The inn serves this to guests at breakfast, and it's a delicious alternative to plain old orange juice. You can make it ahead and store it in the refrigerator, but be sure to stir it well before serving.

1 (48-ounce) can pineapple juice

1 (12-ounce) can defrosted frozen orange juice
  concentrate

1 (12-ounce) can cream of coconut

7 cups water

MIX all of the ingredients in a 1-gallon container. Chill and serve.

VIRGINIA SWEET

sserves 4

THIS RECIPE MAKES a lovely dessert coffee or luncheon coffee.

1 egg white

¾ cup heavy cream

1 teaspoon vanilla extract

4 cups freshly brewed strong, rich coffee

Unsweetened cocoa powder, for dusting (optional)

IN A MEDIUM BOWL, beat the egg white until soft peaks form. Add the cream and vanilla and beat until stiff peaks form. Place one-quarter of the mixture in the bottom of each coffee mug and fill with coffee. When the cream rises, dust the top with cocoa powder and serve.

dandelion root coffee

Coffee was expensive in the early days, so mountain folks found very creative ways to brew what little coffee they did have. Dandelion root coffee is really quite good tasting. When you try this, be sure to find dandelions that haven't been sprayed with herbicides or pesticides.

To make dandelion root coffee, you'll need dandelion roots, washed and cut. Use a shovel to dig the roots because the roots are taproots and can go as deep as 2 feet in good soil. In the early spring and late fall, the roots are at their nutritional height. Look for large plants because they have the fattest roots. It takes about a 5-gallon bucket of roots to make 4 quarts of roasted roots, or 10 gallons of coffee. One good day's work can supply a year's worth of coffee.

To wash the roots, put the bucket near the garden hose, fill it with water, and swish the roots around to loosen the dirt. Pour out the water and start all over again; keep going until you have a nice clean bucket of roots. Take the bucket into the kitchen and, using a large, heavy knife, cut them into chunks. When you get them all cut up, wash them again, and repeat until the water runs clear.

Now place kitchen towels on the counter. Take the chunky roots, about 1 cup at a time, and put them in a food processor. Process on high until they make a coarse mixture. Dump the mixture on the towels and repeat until all the roots are processed. Let them drain on the towels for about an hour.

Preheat the oven to 250°F. Place the dry dandelion roots on baking sheets or in a roasting pan and bake until the roots are brown and brittle, about 2 hours. Leave the oven door slightly ajar so that the moisture can escape, and stir the roots occasionally.

Allow the roots to cool completely, then process once more into a coarse meal. Cool the meal and store it in tightly sealed jars.

To prepare the dandelion root coffee, add about 2 tablespoons to your usual coffee grounds and brew as you normally would, or try a whole pot of dandelion root coffee. Be sure to have sugar and cream handy. This coffee is a little bitter.

---

recipe for "warshing" clothes

Years ago an Alabama grandmother gave a new bride the following recipe for washing clothes:

"BUILD a fire in backyard to heat a kettle of rain water. Set your tubs so smoke won't blow in your eyes if the wind is pert. Shave one hole cake of lie soap in boilin' water.

SORT things, make 3 piles: 1 pile white, 1 pile colored, 1 pile work britches and rags.

TO make starch, stir flour in cool water to smooth, then thin it down with boiling water.

TAKE white things and rub dirty spots on the board. Scrub hard and then boil. Rub colored things but don't boil. Just wrench and starch.

TAKE things out of kettle with broom handle, then wrench, and starch.

HANG the old rags on fence. Spread tea towels on the grass. Pour the wrench water on the flower bed. Scrub the porch with the hot soapy water. Turn the tubs upside down.

GO put on a clean, pretty dress, smooth yo' hair with hair combs. Brew a nice cup o' tea, sit and rock a spell, and count your blessings."

WINTER SPICED COFFEE

serves 8

THIS IS A GOOD PARTY COFFEE or after-dinner coffee. Adjust the ingredients as you like and brew it in a coffee urn.

---

8 tablespoons ground coffee

30 whole cloves

Zest of 1 orange

Zest of 1 lemon

¼ teaspoon ground nutmeg

4 teaspoons sugar

8 cups water

PLACE the coffee, cloves, zests, nutmeg, and sugar in the brewing basket of your coffeemaker. Add the water and brew according to the manufacturer's instructions.

rye coffee

During the Civil War, coffee was very hard to come by in the South, as is explained in this newspaper letter dated September 9, 1861, from the *Savannah (GA) Republican*.

"Mr. Editor: Thinking that your readers would be interested in hearing the news from upper Georgia, I herewith submit you. . . . Sugar and coffee are getting scarce and high. The sugar we are learning to dispense with, and we have an excellent substitute for coffee, very cheap and abundant. It is rye—we have been using it in our family for six weeks, and I think it equally as healthy, and as palatable as the Rio. It is prepared in the same way as coffee, being browned and parched, and afterwards ground fine. So you see as far as coffee is concerned, we don't care a straw about Lincoln's blockade. But, sir, coffee is not the only article we have learned to do without. Our fair daughters are busying themselves in preparing homespun for their dresses, and for their brothers and husbands. Many an old spinning wheel and handloom have been put to work anew, to help in maintaining Southern independence; Yankee tweeds, casimers, and broadcloths, also calicos, ginghams, and delaines will soon go a begging. . . . Gwinnett."

OLD-FASHIONED ROOT BEER

makes about eight 2-liter bottles

ONE SUMMER, WHEN MY FATHER was a young boy, he decided to make root beer. Offers of help from my grandmother were politely rejected, as this was going to be his project. He set up the operation in the basement, painstakingly putting together and bottling the concoction. A few days later, the family was sitting down to dinner when they heard an explosion. Running to the basement, they discovered corks popping and the walls covered in root beer. That should have been the end of his great root beer enterprise, but my mother informs me that, once married, he continued to "blow up" one root beer batch after another.

For this recipe, you'll need eight 2-liter plastic or glass bottles and eight corks. You'll also need a kitchen funnel. Plan to spend a Saturday afternoon making this root beer as a family project. Doesn't a root beer float sound good?

---

8 quarts plus 8 quarts water

2 tablespoons minced fresh ginger

2 tablespoons minced dandelion root

¼ cup juniper berries, crushed

2 tablespoons essence of sassafras extract

¼ cup chopped fresh wintergreen

5 pounds sugar

1 cake compressed yeast

STERILIZE the bottles in hot sudsy water, then rinse them in hot water and invert them on paper towels to dry.

IN A LARGE ENAMELED POT over medium heat, boil 8 quarts of water. Add the ginger, dandelion root, juniper berries, sassafras, and wintergreen. Cover and let it boil slowly for 20 minutes. Strain the liquid through a flannel bag or cheesecloth and return it to the pot, and then turn off the heat. Add the sugar and remaining 8 quarts of water, stirring to blend.

Let the pot stand until the liquid cools to lukewarm.

DISSOLVE the yeast in ¼ cup of water, and then add it to the pot, stirring to blend. Allow the liquid to settle for 15 minutes, and then strain it once more.

USING a kitchen funnel, carefully fill each bottle while holding it in a tilted position, stopping about 2 inches from the top. You don't want to shake it up. Once each bottle is full, cork it tightly.

LET the bottles sit in a warm room for 6 hours, and then move the bottles to a cool place to store them. Chill each bottle before serving.

NOTE: *It is very important to keep everything clean. Bacteria can easily contaminate your root beer and make it go bad. Along the same lines, always keep it covered so that your root beer is not exposed to air.*

SOUTHERN MILK PUNCH

serves 4

THIS IS A TRADITIONAL party punch throughout the southern Appalachian region.

---

3 cups vanilla ice cream

½ cup bourbon

1 tablespoon vanilla extract

Freshly grated nutmeg, for serving

COMBINE the ice cream, bourbon, and vanilla in a blender and blend until smooth. Pour the punch into glasses and sprinkle each with grated nutmeg before serving.

EGGNOG

serves 20

THIS IS A VERY GOOD EGGNOG! The original recipe came from Alabama. It will keep for several weeks in a tightly covered container in the refrigerator.

2½ cups bourbon

1½ cups dark rum

1½ cups brandy

4 quarts eggnog (Southern Comfort brand preferred)

1 gallon eggnog ice cream, at room temperature

½ teaspoon vanilla extract

Ground nutmeg, for dusting

IN A LARGE BOWL, mix together the bourbon, rum, brandy, and eggnog. Add the ice cream and blend well, and then stir in the vanilla, mixing well. Pour the mixture into individual serving glasses and dust the top of each glass with nutmeg before serving.

MAMMY WILLIAMS'S DANDELION WINE

makes almost 1 gallon

THIS RECIPE IS FROM the Home Place Bed and Breakfast Inn in Mooresburg, Tennessee. Built in the early 1800s as a log cabin, the Home Place has been owned by Priscilla Rogers's family since then. Many generations have left their mark on the home by renovating it to meet their needs, and today it is a cozy yet spacious place. Mammy was Carrie Moore Williams, the granddaughter of Hugh Moore, who founded Mooresburg. Carrie owned the Mooresburg Springs Hotel and ran a boarding home where the Home Place is today. It takes about two months to make this wine, but it's an old southern Appalachian recipe and very good. You will need a 1-gallon crock or plastic bucket for this recipe.

---

12 cups dandelions and stems, roots trimmed

3 sliced lemons

1 cup raisins

3 pounds sugar

IN A LARGE POT, cover the dandelions and stems with boiling water and let stand for 24 hours.

STRAIN the liquid into a 1-gallon crock, and then add the lemons, raisins, and sugar. Stir to blend and cover with cheesecloth. Let the mixture stand for 12 days (in a very cool place).

STRAIN the solids out and let the liquid sit in a warm place for 6 weeks.

POUR the liquid into sterilized bottles, seal the bottles with corks, and store them in a cool, dry place.

HOMEMADE APPALACHIAN WINE

makes 4 to 5 gallons

LARRY WARD OF SEVIERVILLE, TENNESSEE, gave me this recipe. He is a fifth-generation woodworker and artisan, born in the hills of east Tennessee. "The amount of wine you make depends on the size of the crock you use to make it in," Larry tells me. Some folks make small batches and others make enough for their friends and neighbors. It just depends on how much fruit is available. For this recipe you will need a 5-gallon ceramic crock or plastic bucket, with the former being preferred.

---

10 pounds fruit (any fruit that will ferment, such as Muscadine or Scuppernong grapes, watermelon, peaches, apples, strawberries, raspberries, blackberries, gooseberries, or plums), plus extra if needed to fill the crock three-quarters full

7 pounds sugar

2 gallons filtered water

WASH the fruit and cut it into thick slices if necessary (cut grapes or strawberries in half). Put the fruit into the large crock, peels or rind and all. Pour in the sugar, covering the fruit, and stir to blend.

FILL the crock to 4 to 5 inches from the top with water and stir to blend the contents. Cover the crock with cheesecloth and let it sit in a cool, dark place for 2 to 3 months, checking the mixture every once in a while to see how the fermentation is going. The fruit will bubble and fizz as it breaks down into a liquid. A vintner would use modern scientific methods for regulating the fermentation process; it'll be a little harder for you to tell. Just because the mixture has stopped bubbling or fizzing does not mean it's through fermenting, which is why the crock is left for 3 months. That should be enough time for fermentation to stop on its own.

WHEN fermentation has stopped, strain the wine through cheesecloth into another container and then pour it into sterilized bottles. Seal the bottles with corks and store them in a cool, dry place.

grapes and appalachian wine

One most likely doesn't think of table wines when one thinks of the mountains. However, summer grapes are very important to southern Appalachia and to wildlife. These high-producing grapes are widely spread throughout the region.

The settlers to the mountains made their own wines by a long process of fermentation in crocks. Muscadine grapes and their Scuppernong variety, and other fruits, were and still are very popular "wine fixins'."

There are two major wine-producing areas and a few smaller pockets in the southern Appalachians: Virginia's Shenandoah Valley, where the limestone and sandstone deposits make the soil excellent for growing grapes, and North Carolina's Yadkin Valley. Most of the original Muscadine and Scuppernong grape varieties that grew wild for centuries have been replaced with the cultivation of Chardonnay, Merlot, and Cabernet Sauvignon grapes. There are also wineries in southeastern West Virginia and eastern Tennessee that produce some very aromatic wines. The fertile mountain soil produces a variety of fine wines and the visitor is always welcome to do a little tasting.

HOMEMADE WINE

Making homemade wine is a lengthy process and, in southern Appalachia, the knowledge is passed down. There are wine-making kits available with all the chemicals and supplies needed, but in the mountains, folks make it the old-fashioned way. I've learned two valuable things about mountain wine. First, if a little mold grows at the top of the crock, "Just scrape it off. It ain't gonna hurt no one." Second, always use a cork. A cork allows the wine to expand, or "breathe." If you use a screw top, it could explode.

Most folks save old wine bottles or get used ones from restaurants, remove the labels, and sterilize them for use. Store the bottled wine in a cool, dark place such as a basement or cupboard or old-fashioned springhouse.

MINT JULEP

serves 1

THE FIVE-ACRE ASHFORD ESTATE, overlooking Main Street in Watkinsville, Georgia, had been in the same family for more than one hundred years. Completely surrounded and secluded by a border of magnolias, redbuds, and pines, the 1893 Victorian manor house, cottage, gazebo, and acres of landscaped gardens all terrace down to a pool, open woods and creek beyond. In the summer, you can listen to concerts on the lawn or watch a Shakespearean play. The classic southern mint julep calls for a quarter-shot of bitters, but being transplanted Yankees, the owners of the Ashford Estate decided to substitute the Italian liqueur Campari for variety. They feel it enhances the color of the liquid as it mingles with the ice and mint, and Campari's complexity of bitter flavors provides this southern staple with a little continental sophistication. Of course, this is frowned on by any traditional southerner, but a little change now and then adds spice to life. As you can see below, the rest of the recipe is quite traditional.

---

1 shot bourbon

¼ shot Campari

3 shots simple syrup (see Note)

1 mint sprig, plus 1 for garnish

1 pewter julep cup

Confectioners' sugar, for dusting

1 small cocktail straw

1 rocking chair

1 front porch

1 lovely southern afternoon or evening

IN A SMALL PITCHER, stir together the bourbon, Campari, simple syrup, and 1 mint sprig. Fill the julep cup with crushed ice and pour the mixture over the ice. Garnish with a mint sprig and dust with confectioners' sugar.

ADD a small cocktail straw and enjoy while sitting in a rocking chair on your favorite porch.

NOTE: *To make the simple syrup, combine 1 part water with 1 part granulated sugar and boil the mixture over medium heat, stirring until the sugar dissolves. Move the pan off the heat to cool for a bit, and then chill the mixture before using it.*

Moonshine

The production of whiskey in the southern Appalachian area has been going on since the first European settlers arrived. Early moonshine was used to pay debts or for bartering. In 1794, the government expected folks to pay a tax on homemade whiskey. Settlers considered this a federal intrusion into their freedom, and the Whiskey Rebellion broke out along the western frontier. A lot of people started making their own liquor, or moonshine, in secret. During the Civil War, the government once again taxed whiskey to fund northern troops. After the Civil War, the Revenue Bureau of the Treasury Department was formed and the "Revenuers" were sent to hunt out and prosecute unlawful distilling. They were sent everywhere, regardless of state lines or laws. In 1876, Senator Zebulon Vance campaigned against the revenue laws, stating, "The time has come when an honest man can't take an honest drink without having a gang of revenue officers after him." While some distillers complied and shut down their stills, others did not. In 1894, the government raised the tax to $1.10 per gallon of whiskey, and the result was a huge increase in moonshine stills and production. The war against illegal whiskey was on. Revenuers covered the mountains and back roads of southern Appalachia in an attempt to stop moonshine production. A Revenuer was easy to spot because he was most likely the only outsider in the area. Families guarded their stills with guns, and many battles ended up with dead on both sides.

With the passage of the Eighteenth Amendment to the Constitution in January 1919, Prohibition brought a boom time to moonshiners. Farmers in Appalachia and other remote parts of the country found they could make more money turning their corn crops into moonshine when grain profits on the general market weren't good. Moonshine stills that had once operated only for personal use ran twenty-four hours a day, producing "shine" for the illegal whiskey trade. When Prohibition ended in 1933, that wasn't the end of moonshine running. As late as the 1960s, moonshine was being carried out of the mountains and into large cities.

In the 1960s, Bobby Rae, I'll call him, was a young man of eighteen when he signed on to "run shine" from Sevierville, Tennessee, into Knoxville, Tennessee, nearly thirty miles. The local "boss" would sell the shine and then the runner would have to deliver it. As Bobby Rae tells it, "We drove at night with the headlights off so no one could see us. I'd be drivin' down Chapman highway [a two-lane winding road in those days], a hundred mile an hour, and I'd look in the rear view and there'd be a Revenuer right on my tail. I didn't want to go to jail so I'd have to outrun 'em. We was drivin' special cars. The shine was in a tank in the back and if it got too bad, I could pull a lever and it would go all over the road. There was another tank with oil in it. If I pulled that lever, a big slick would cover the road and the Revenuers would lose control. I could never bring myself to do that, though. Didn't want to cause nobody's death. They paid us one hundred and fifty dollars a run. That was real good money back then." When asked why he quit, Bobby replied, " I was makin' a run one night and goin' about one hundred. A Revenuer came right up to my bumper and banged into me trying to get me to go off the road. That was enough to let me know he meant business. That scared me out of the runnin' business."

MAKIN' MOONSHINE

Even though there remain mountain stills at work, making moonshine for sale, it's illegal. Some folks (tourists from up north) came up into this holler a few years back and asked one of my neighbors, "Where's the still?" My neighbor, deciding to give them a show, went into his house and returned with a shotgun. Those folks were gone back down the road in a flash, and my neighbor had a good laugh.

To make moonshine, you start with a mash, which is a mixture of grain, sugar, water, and yeast, which ferments to produce alcohol. The grain is virtually always corn, so the product is often called "corn liquor." Other names for it are "corn whiskey," "mountain dew," "white lightning," and "shine."

When the mash quits bubbling, it is cooked in a still and the steam is captured in a barrel filled with water. The steam is allowed to cool and condense as it runs though a long copper coil submerged in another barrel that is constantly cooled with water brought in from a nearby stream. The clear liquor condenses and drips from the bottom of the barrel into a catch can or half-gallon glass jars.

The liquor is tested for alcohol content, or proof, by adding gunpowder to it and igniting the mixture. If it blows up, its proof is established at somewhere between 100 and 200 proof, or 50 to 100 percent alcohol. There has been many a moonlit night that I've heard a small explosion here and there in the mountains. The way I see it, "they was either amakin' shine or chasing a possum."

chapter 10

COUNTRY STORE

GRANDMA'S FRESH TABLE PICKLES

serves 4 to 6

THIS EASY RECIPE IS from the Blue Mountain Mist Inn in Sevierville, Tennessee. The property that the inn sits on has been in the family for a very long time, and many of the dishes they serve are old family recipes.

———————◆———————

¼ cup white vinegar

2 tablespoons freshly squeezed lemon juice

2 tablespoons sugar

¼ teaspoon celery seed

Pinch of salt and freshly ground black pepper

2 large cucumbers, sliced

1 medium white or yellow onion, finely chopped

IN A LARGE BOWL, blend the vinegar, lemon juice, sugar, celery seed, salt, and pepper. Add the cucumbers and onion and stir to coat.

COVER and let it sit in the refrigerator for at least 30 minutes to 1 hour, but preferably longer. The longer the pickles sit, the stronger the flavor will be. Transfer, juices and all, to a pretty bowl and serve.

SWEET AND SOUR CUCUMBERS

serves 4 to 6

THIS IS A SOUL FOOD RECIPE from the southern Appalachian region of northern Alabama. They are delicious. They're good mixed with any kind of beans—especially with fresh-cut green beans.

———————◆———————

3 large cucumbers, peeled and sliced ⅛ inch thick

2 large red onions, sliced

¼ cup cider vinegar

½ cup plus 1 teaspoon sugar

1 teaspoon salt

4½ cups water

IN A LARGE CONTAINER with a lid, combine the cucumbers and onions.

IN A MEASURING CUP, combine the vinegar, sugar, salt, and water and stir well. Pour the mixture over the cucumbers and mix well. Cover the container and refrigerate it for at least 2 hours before serving.

GREEN TOMATO PICKLES

makes nine 1-pint jars

THIS MELUNGEON RECIPE is an old southern Appalachian favorite. To folks in other regions of the country, green tomato pickles may seem strange, but they are a popular dish. They take some time to make, but these pickles are worth the wait. Use them on a hamburger or sandwich, by themselves, or in salads. Delicious!

16 cups (1 gallon) thinly sliced green tomatoes

¼ cup plus ¼ cup pickling salt

2 cups thinly sliced onion

3 cups firmly packed brown sugar

4 cups white vinegar (5 percent acidity)

1 tablespoon whole cloves

1 tablespoon whole allspice berries

1 tablespoon celery seed

1 tablespoon mustard seed

PLACE the tomatoes in a bowl, sprinkle with ¼ cup of the pickling salt, and stir. Place the onion in another bowl, sprinkle with the remaining ¼ cup pickling salt, and stir. Cover both bowls and let them sit at room temperature for 4 to 6 hours, and then drain off and discard the liquid.

IN A LARGE SAUCEPAN or pot over medium heat, combine the brown sugar and vinegar and stir until the sugar is dissolved. Tie the cloves, allspice, celery seed, and mustard seed in a piece of cheesecloth or a spice bag and add the bag to the vinegar mixture. Stir in the drained tomatoes and onions.

BRING the mixture to a boil, and then reduce the heat and simmer for 30 minutes, stirring as needed to prevent scorching. The tomatoes should be tender and transparent when properly cooked. Remove the pan from the heat and discard the spice bag. Spoon the tomatoes into hot sterilized pint jars and cover them with the vinegar solution, leaving ½ inch of headspace at the tops of the jars. Wipe the rims of the jars with a clean, damp cloth to remove any drips and seal the jars tightly. Process them in a boiling water bath for 10 minutes, following your home canner manufacturer's instructions.

SPICED PEACHES

makes six 1-pint jars

SPICED PEACHES ARE A REAL TREAT! I love them. They can be served as a side to beef, lamb, and pork. They're also good by themselves or over vanilla ice cream. Traditionally, the pits are left in the whole peaches, which make a lovely presentation. However, you may remove the pits and halve the peaches before cooking if you wish. They look a little "mushy" if you remove the pits.

---

6 pounds medium sweet peaches

2¾ cups cider vinegar

1⅓ cups water

8 cups sugar

4 cinnamon sticks, broken in half

4 teaspoons whole cloves

WASH the peaches well, peel them, and place them in a bowl. (The easiest way to peel a peach is to dip the fruit in boiling water for 30 to 60 seconds. Remove from the water using a slotted spoon and put into a large bowl or pot of cold water and ice. The skins will easily slide off.) Cut out any brown spots. Traditionally, you leave the pits in, but you can halve them and pit them if you want.

IN A LARGE POT on medium-low heat, mix the vinegar, water, and sugar. Raise the heat to medium and cook, stirring, until the sugar dissolves. Add the cinnamon sticks and cloves to the pot and bring the mixture to a boil. Cover the pot and let it boil for 5 minutes, then uncover it and boil for 5 minutes more. Add the peaches to the pot and bring the mixture back to a boil, and then turn the heat down to a simmer. Let the syrup simmer for 10 minutes.

SPOON the peaches into hot sterilized pint jars to about three-quarters full. Next, spoon the liquid mixture over the peaches, leaving ¼ inch of headspace. Make sure there is at least one piece of cinnamon in each jar. Wipe the rims of the jars with a clean, damp cloth to remove any drips and seal the jars tightly. Process the peaches in a hot water bath for 10 minutes, following your home canner manufacturer's instructions.

NOTE: *Canned peaches have a shelf life of 1½ to 2 years.*

PEAR RELISH

makes 5 to 6 pints

THIS IS A SOUL FOOD RECIPE from the southern Appalachian region of northern Alabama. It's a good relish for vegetables.

———————————

4 cups plus 4 cups vinegar

4 cups sugar

1 tablespoon ground turmeric

3 tablespoons dry mustard

3 tablespoons all-purpose flour

2 tablespoons salt

4 tablespoons mustard seed

16 cups (1 gallon) finely chopped pears (processed in a blender or food processor into small chunks, then drained)

12 cups ground onions (process in blender or food processor into small chunks)

8 green bell peppers, seeded and diced

4 red bell peppers, seeded and diced

2 hot fresh chiles of your choice, seeded and finely minced

4 cups drained and chopped dill pickles

IN A LARGE SAUCEPAN over low heat, combine 4 cups of the vinegar with the sugar, turmeric, dry mustard, flour, salt, and mustard seed. Cook until the sugar dissolves.

ADD the remaining 4 cups vinegar, the pears, onions, bell peppers, hot chiles, and pickles. Bring to a boil, stirring, and let it boil for 20 minutes.

POUR the mixture into hot sterilized jars. Wipe the rims of the jars with a clean, damp cloth to remove any drips and seal the jars tightly. Process the jars in a hot water bath for 10 minutes, following your home canner manufacturer's instructions.

BLUEBERRY MARMALADE

makes 6 half-pint jars

IF YOU HAVEN'T TRIED blueberry marmalade, then you've missed an old-fashioned treat. Here in the mountains blueberries can be found in the wild or at farms that sell direct to the public. Picking your own berries ensures that you have the biggest, juiciest ingredients for your homemade marmalade.

1 medium orange

1 medium lemon

¾ cup water

⅛ teaspoon baking soda

4 cups fresh blueberries, crushed

5 cups sugar

1 (6-ounce) package liquid pectin

PEEL the orange and lemon. Finely chop the rinds and place them in a large saucepan. Chop the orange and lemon pulp and set aside.

ADD the water and baking soda to the chopped rind in the saucepan and bring it to a boil over medium-low heat. Turn the heat to low and simmer for 10 minutes, stirring occasionally. Add the chopped orange and lemon pulp, blueberries, and sugar and return to a boil, and then reduce the heat and simmer for 5 minutes.

REMOVE the saucepan from the heat and let cool for 5 minutes. Add the pectin and bring the mixture back to a boil over medium heat. Boil for 1 minute, stirring constantly.

REMOVE the saucepan from the heat and skim off the foam with a metal spoon.

POUR the mixture into hot sterilized pint jars, leaving ¼ inch of headspace at the tops. Wipe the rims of the jars with a clean, damp cloth to remove any drips and seal the jars tightly. Place the jars in a boiling water bath for 10 minutes, following your home canner manufacturer's instructions.

DANDELION JELLY

makes 6 half-pint jars

DANDELIONS ARE NOT WEEDS. They are wild vegetables, and all parts of the plant are useable. According to the USDA, dandelions are more nutritious than broccoli or spinach. However, do not use dandelions unless you are sure they have not been sprayed with weed killers or other chemicals. The people of the southern highlands used dandelions in everything from wine (see page 181) to jams and jellies as well as serving them as a vegetable. They have a delicate flavor and are still enjoyed in southern Appalachian dishes today.

---

4 cups packed dandelion blossoms (yellow parts)

3 cups water

4½ cups sugar

1 (1.75-ounce) package powdered pectin

2 tablespoons freshly squeezed lemon juice

1 or 2 drops yellow food coloring (optional)

PICK over the dandelion blossoms to make sure there are no green parts with the yellow blossoms. The green parts have a bitter flavor. Shred the blossoms into small pieces. In a large saucepan, bring the water to a boil over medium heat. Add about a cup of the dandelion blossom shreds, stir, and lower the heat and simmer for 10 minutes.

STRAIN the liquid into a bowl or a separate pot, pressing the blossoms to get as much liquid as possible out of them. Put the strained liquid back into the large saucepan. Continue simmering and straining the blossoms in batches (about 1 cup per batch) until all the blossoms are used up.

ADD more water to the saucepan to make 3 cups. Strain the liquid through a fine-mesh strainer or a coffee filter to remove all particles. Add the sugar, pectin, lemon juice, and food coloring and bring to a roiling boil, stirring until the sugar dissolves. Continue the roiling boil for 1 minute, and then skim off any bubbles or foam with a metal spoon.

POUR the mixture into hot sterilized pint jars, leaving ¼ inch of headspace at the tops. Wipe the rims of the jars with a clean, damp cloth to remove any drips and seal the jars tightly. Place the jars in a boiling water bath for 5 minutes, following your home canner manufacturer's instructions.

NOTE: *If you can't collect enough dandelion blossoms at one time, you can freeze what you collect until you have enough.*

CORNCOB JELLY

makes 6 half-pint jars

THIS OLD CHEROKEE RECIPE has become a country classic. The southern highlanders weren't ones to waste anything, and that included the corncob. Not only did the corncob make a fine smoking pipe and food for livestock, but it also made this delightful golden-colored jelly, which tastes a little like plum jelly. You can also make smaller batches and store it in the refrigerator instead of preserving it if you plan to use it right away.

---

12 ears fresh red or yellow corn on the cob

4 cups water

4 cups sugar

1 (3-ounce) package liquid pectin

Canning wax, for sealing

CLEAN the corncobs by scraping off the kernels. Save the kernels for other uses. Break the cobs in half.

IN A LARGE POT, heat the water over medium heat. Add the cleaned cobs, cover the pot, and bring it to a low boil. Boil the cobs for 30 minutes, and then remove them from the pot and strain the liquid through cheesecloth. Return the liquid to the pot and discard the cobs. If necessary, add enough water to the liquid to make 3 cups.

TURN the heat to medium and stir in the sugar. Bring the mixture to a boil, stirring constantly, and cook until the sugar dissolves. Stir the pectin into the liquid mixture and cook for 1 more minute.

REMOVE the pan from the heat and skim off any bubbles and foam with a metal spoon. Spoon the mixture into hot sterilized pint jars. Seal each jar with canning wax, according to the manufacturer's directions.

SWEET POTATO JAM

makes about two 1-pint jars or 4 half-pint jars

SWEET POTATO JAM? You've probably never heard of it before, or just maybe you've encountered it on your travels. It's delicious. It's very good on toast, scones, and muffins. This is a delicate jam that should be stored in the refrigerator after canning and used within 5 days of opening.

————◆—◆————

2 tablespoons freshly squeezed lemon juice

1½ pounds yellow sweet potatoes

4 cups water

2 cups sugar

Grated zest of 1 large orange

1 cinnamon stick

4 whole cloves

¼ teaspoon ground nutmeg

¼ teaspoon vanilla extract

FILL a medium bowl halfway to three-quarters full of cold water and add the lemon juice. Peel and chop the sweet potatoes and put the pieces into the bowl as you go so that they do not turn brown.

IN A LARGE SAUCEPAN over medium heat, combine the 4 cups water, the sugar, orange zest, cinnamon stick, cloves, and nutmeg. Bring to a low boil, stirring constantly, and let cook until the sugar dissolves. Turn the heat to low and remove the cinnamon stick and cloves.

ADD the sweet potato pieces to the pot and cook, stirring occasionally, for 30 minutes, or until the sweet potatoes are cooked very well. If necessary, mash them a little and then use a wooden spoon to stir until well blended. Add the vanilla and blend again. You want the consistency of jam, so if necessary add more water 1 tablespoon at a time, stirring after each addition.

WHEN the jam has reached the desired consistency, spoon it into hot sterilized jars. Wipe the rims of the jars with a clean, damp cloth to remove any drips and seal the jars tightly. Turn the jars upside down on a towel for 10 minutes, and then turn them upright and let them cool completely. Store the jam in the refrigerator until ready to use.

STRAWBERRY SYRUP

makes three 1-pint jars

———◆◆◆———

8 cups crushed fresh strawberries

¼ cup freshly squeezed lemon juice

3 cups sugar

1 cup light corn syrup

PLACE the strawberries in a 4- to 6-quart pot and bring them to a boil over medium heat, stirring occasionally. Pour the berries into a bowl covered with a double thickness of dampened cheesecloth. Let the juice drip for at least 2 hours. There should be 3 to 4 cups of juice.

RETURN the strawberry juice to the pot and add the lemon juice, sugar, and corn syrup. Bring the mixture to a rolling boil over high heat, stirring constantly, and boil for 1 minute.

POUR the syrup into hot sterilized pint jars, leaving ¼ inch of headspace at the tops. Wipe the rims of the jars with a clean, damp cloth to remove any syrup and seal the jars tightly. Process the jars in a hot water bath for 10 minutes, following your home canner manufacturer's instructions.

PECAN SYRUP

makes 4 half-pint jars

———◆◆◆———

⅓ cup firmly packed dark brown sugar

1 cup coarsely chopped pecans

2 cups dark corn syrup

½ cup water

1 teaspoon vanilla extract

IN A BLENDER or food processor, combine the brown sugar and pecans and process until the nuts are finely ground.

IN A MEDIUM SAUCEPAN over medium heat, combine the sugar-nut mixture, corn syrup, and water. Bring to a boil, stirring constantly, and boil for 1 minute. Remove the pan from the heat and stir in the vanilla.

POUR the syrup into hot sterilized half-pint jars, leaving ¼ inch of headspace at the tops. Wipe the rims of the jars with a clean, damp cloth to remove any syrup and seal the jars tightly. Place the jars in a boiling water bath for 10 minutes, following your home canner manufacturer's instructions.

BLACKBERRY SYRUP

makes about 6 cups

---

1 ½ quarts fresh ripe blackberries

2 cups sugar

1 tablespoon freshly squeezed lemon juice

1 teaspoon unsalted butter

2 cups light corn syrup

WASH the berries and process them a little at a time in a blender, food processor, or juicer until they are completely pulverized.

STRAIN the berry pulp through a fine-mesh sieve and measure out 2¼ cups of juice. Place the juice in a 6- or 8-quart pot over medium heat and bring to a boil, stirring occasionally. Add the sugar, lemon juice, and butter, stirring until the sugar dissolves. Add the corn syrup and blend well. Reduce the heat to low and simmer for 5 minutes.

POUR the syrup into hot sterilized jars, leaving ¼ inch of headspace at the tops. Wipe the rims of the jars with a clean, damp cloth to remove any syrup and seal the jars tightly. Place the jars in a boiling water bath for 10 minutes, following your home canner manufacturer's instructions.

CINNAMON SYRUP

makes 6 half-pint jars

---

3 cups sugar

1 tablespoon ground cinnamon

6 cups water

⅓ cup freshly squeezed orange juice

IN A SAUCEPAN over medium heat, combine the sugar, cinnamon, water, and orange juice. Bring to boil, stirring constantly to dissolve the sugar. Boil for 10 minutes without stirring.

POUR the syrup into hot sterilized jars, leaving ¼ inch of headspace at the tops. Wipe the rims of the jars with a clean, damp cloth to remove any syrup and seal the jars tightly. Place the jars in a boiling water bath for 10 minutes, following your home canner manufacturer's instructions.

Sources and Resources

ORGANIZATIONS

Melungeon Heritage Association
PO Box 4042
Wise, Virginia 24292
www.melungeon.org

Appalshop
91 Madison Avenue
Whitesburg, Kentucky 41858
(606) 633-0108
www.appalshop.org

International Storytelling Center
116 Main Street
Jonesborough, Tennessee 37659
(800) 952-8392
www.storytellingcenter.net

Birthplace of Country Music Alliance
510 Cumberland Street, Suite 103
Bristol, Virginia 24201
(276) 645-0111
www.birthplaceofcountrymusic.org

SELECTED SOUTHERN APPALACHIAN BED-AND-BREAKFAST INNS

ALABAMA

Columbus Street Inn
1043 Columbus Street West
Fayette, Alabama 35555
(205) 932-4411
www.columbusstreetinn.com

The Lodge on Gorham's Bluff
101 Gorham Drive
Gorham's Bluff
Pisgah, Alabama 35765
(256) 451-8439
www.gorhamsbluff.com

Mentone Inn
6139 Alabama, Highway 117
Mentone, Alabama 35984
(800) 455-7470 or (256) 634-4836
www.mentoneinn.com

GEORGIA

Ashford Manor
5 Harden Hill Road
Watkinsville, Georgia 30677
(706) 769-2633
www.ambedandbreakfast.com

Brady Inn Bed and Breakfast
250 North Second Street
Madison, Georgia 30650
(866) 770-0773
www.bradyinn.com

Henson Cove Place Bed & Breakfast
1137 Car Miles Road
Hiawassee, Georgia 30546
(800) 714-5542
www.henson-cove-place.com

Hidden Valley Bed & Breakfast
441 Mull Road
Hiawassee, Georgia 30546
(866) 850-6274
www.hiddenvalleybandb.com

Sylvan Falls Bed & Breakfast Inn
156 Taylor's Chapel Road
Rabun Gap, Georgia 30568
(706) 746-7138
www.iloveinns.com

KENTUCKY

1869 Shaker Tavern Bed & Breakfast
U.S. 73
South Union, Kentucky 42283
(800) 929-8701
www.shakermuseum.com

Farmhouse Inn
735 Taylor Branch Road
Parkers Lake, Kentucky 42634
(606) 376-7383
www.farmhouseinnbb.com

Federal Grove Inn
475 East Main Street
Auburn, Kentucky 42206
(270) 542-6106
www.bbonline.com/ky/fedgrove

NORTH CAROLINA

4½ Street Inn
55 4½ Street
Highlands, North Carolina 28741
(888) 799-4464
www.4andahalfstinn.com

Angel's Landing Inn
94 Campbell Street
Murphy, North Carolina 28906
(828) 835-8877
www.angelslandinginn.com

Applewood Manor
62 Cumberland Circle
Asheville, North Carolina 28801
(800) 442-2197
www.applewoodmanor.com

Azalea Inn
149 Azalea Circle
Banner Elk, North Carolina 28604
(888) 898-2743
www.azalea-inn.com

Buffalo Tavern Bed and Breakfast
958 West Buffalo Road
West Jefferson, North Carolina 28694
(877) 615-9678
www.buffalotavern.com

Buttonwood Inn
50 Admiral Drive
Franklin, North Carolina 28734
(828) 369-8985
www.buttonwoodbb.com

Folkestone Inn
101 Folkestone Road
Bryson City, North Carolina 28713
(828) 488-2730
www.folkestoneinn.com

Greystone Inn
Greystone Lane
Lake Toxaway, North Carolina 28747
(800) 824-5766
www.greystoneinn.com

Ponder Cove Inn
1067 Ponder Creek Road
Mars Hill, North Carolina 28754
(866) 689-7304
www.pondercove.com

Terrell House Bed & Breakfast
109 Robertson Street
Burnsville, North Carolina 28714
(888) 682-4505
www.terrellhousebandb.com

Chalet Inn
285 Lone Oak Drive
Bryson City, North Carolina 28725
(800) 789-8024
www.chaletinn.com

Hawkesdene House
381 Phillips Creek Road
Andrews, North Carolina 28901
(800) 447-9549
www.hawkesdene.com

SOUTH CAROLINA

Sunrise Farm Bed & Breakfast
325 Sunrise Drive
Salem, South Carolina 29676
(888) 991-0121
www.bbonline.com/sc/sunrisefarm

Inn at Merridun
100 Merridun Place
Union, South Carolina 29379
(888) 892-6020
www.merridun.com

TENNESSEE

Berry Springs Lodge
2149 Seaton Springs Road
Sevierville, Tennessee 37862
(888) 760-8297
www.berrysprings.com

Blue Mountain Mist Country Inn
1811 Pullen Road
Sevierville, Tennessee 37862
(800) 497-2335
www.bluemountainmist.com

Braeside Inn
115 Ruth Lane
Sevierville, Tennessee 37862
(866) 429-5859
www.braesideinnbb.com

Buckhorn Inn
2140 Tudor Mountain Road
Gatlinburg, Tennessee 37738
(866) 941-0460
www.buckhorninn.com

Calico Inn
757 Ranch Way
Sevierville, Tennessee 37862
(800) 235-1054
www.calico-inn.com

Creekwalk Inn at Whisperwood Farm
166 Middle Creek Road
Cosby, Tennessee 37722
(800) 962-2246
www.whisperwoodretreat.com

Dancing Bear Lodge
137 Apple Valley Way
Townsend, Tennessee 37882
(800) 369-0111
www.dancingbearlodge.com

Fiddlers Glen Bed & Breakfast
104 South Third Avenue
Jonesborough, Tennessee 37659
(423) 913-3259
www.fiddlersglenbnb.com

Fox Manor
1612 Watauga Street
Kingsport, Tennessee 37664
(888) 200-5879
www.foxmanor.com

Grace Hill
1169 Little Round Top Way
Townsend, Tennessee 37882-3434
(866) 448-3070
www.gracehillbandb.com

Home Place Bed & Breakfast Inn
132 Church Lane
Mooresburg, Tennessee 37811
(800) 521-8424
www.bbonline.com/tn/homeplace

Iron Mountain Inn Bed & Breakfast
138 Moreland Drive
Butler Tennessee 37640
(888) 781-2399
www.ironmountaininn.com

Laurel Springs Lodge Bed & Breakfast
204 Hill Street
Gatlinburg, Tennessee 37738
(888) 430-9211
www.laurelspringlodge.com

Prospect Hill Bed & Breakfast
801 West Main Street/Highway 67
Mountain City, Tennessee 37683
(800) 339-5084
www.prospect-hill.com

Tanasi Hill Bed & Breakfast Inn
102 Doughty Avenue
Greeneville, Tennessee 37745
(423) 638-1693
www.bbonline.com/tn/tanasi

Walnut Lane Inn
110 Ridge Road
Lyman, SC 29365
(864) 949-7230
www.walnutlaneinn.com

VIRGINIA

Ambrosia Farm Bed & Breakfast and Pottery
271 Cox Store Road
Floyd, Virginia 24091
(540) 745-6363
www.ambrosiafarm.net

Claiborne House Bed & Breakfast Inn
185 Claiborne Avenue
Rocky Mount, Virginia 24151
(540) 483-4616
www.claibornehouse.net

Clay Corner Inn
401 Clay Street SW
Blacksburg, Virginia 24060
(540) 552-4030
www.claycorner.com

Cripple Creek Bed and Breakfast Cabins
155 Log Cabin Lane
Crockett, Virginia 24323
(276) 686-2000
www.cripplecreekcabins.com

Flo's Hideaway
127 Solar Street
Bristol, Virginia 24201
(276) 644-9805
www.flo-s-hideaway.com

Maison Beliveau Bed & Breakfast
5415 Gallion Ridge Road /
  3860 Rue Maison Beliveau
Blacksburg, Virginia 24060
(540) 961-0505
www.maisonbeliveau.com

Miracle Farm Bed & Breakfast Spa Resort
179 Ida Rose Lane
Floyd, Virginia 24091
(540) 789-2214
www.miraclefarmbnb.com

Mountain Rose Inn
1787 Charity Highway
Woolwine, Virginia 24185
(888) 930-1057
www.mountainrose-inn.com

Rockwood Manor
5189 Rockwood Road
Dublin, Virginia 24084
(540) 674-1328
www.rockwood-manor.com

Collins House Inn
204 West Main Street
Marion, Virginia 24354-2516
(276) 781-0250
www.collinshouseinn.com

SOUTHERN FOOD PRODUCTS AVAILABLE BY MAIL ORDER AND ONLINE

Margaret Holmes Brand
(Southern classic foods)
McCall Farms
Effingham, South Carolina 29541
(800) 277-2012
www.margaretholmes.com

Appalachian Spring Cooperative
(Located in the southern Appalachian highlands of east Tennessee; the cooperative is a member-owned association of farmers and entrepreneurs creating quality, locally produced food and herbal products.)
www.apspringcoop.com

Tennessee T-Cakes
(The ultimate Southern confection, this recipe is over 100 years old. I've been sending T-Cakes to friends for years.)
Tennessee T-Cakes, Inc
200 Hill Avenue, Suite 5
Nashville, Tennessee 37210
(615) 256-3950
(888) 886-3926
www.tntcakes.com

RESOURCES FOR CANNING AND PRESERVING FOODS BY MAIL ORDER AND ONLINE

The USDA Complete Guide to Home Canning
foodsafety.cas.psu.edu/
canningguide.html

Montana State University Extension
Home canning pressures and processing times:
www.msuextension
.org/publications/
HomeHealthandFamily/
MT198329HR.pdf
The extension catalog: www
.extn.msu.montana.edu/
Publications/ESCatalog/
HOMEPublicHomeFood_and_
Nutritionlist.asp?cmd=resetall

National Presto Industries
(Presto canners and parts)
(800) 877-0441
www.gopresto.com

Wisconsin Aluminum Foundry
(All-American Canners)
Consumer Products Division
838 South 16th Street
PO Box 246
Manitowoc, Wisconsin 54221
(920) 682-8627
https://store.wafco.com/
ezmerchant/home.nsf

Alltrista Corporation
(Ball and Kerr canning supplies)
(800) 392-2575
www.freshpreserving.com

Metric Conversions and Equivalents

METRIC CONVERSION FORMULAS

TO CONVERT	MULTIPLY
Ounces to grams	Ounces by 28.35
Pounds to kilograms	Pounds by 0.454
Teaspoons to milliliters	Teaspoons by 4.93
Tablespoons to milliliters	Tablespoons by 14.79
Fluid ounces to milliliters	Fluid ounces by 29.57
Cups to milliliters	Cups by 236.59
Cups to liters	Cups by 0.236
Pints to liters	Pints by 0.473
Quarts to liters	Quarts by 0.946
Gallons to liters	Gallons by 3.785
Inches to centimeters	Inches by 2.54

APPROXIMATE METRIC EQUIVALENTS

VOLUME

¼ teaspoon	1 milliliter
½ teaspoon	2.5 milliliters
¾ teaspoon	4 milliliters
1 teaspoon	5 milliliters
1¼ teaspoons	6 milliliters
1½ teaspoons	7.5 milliliters
1¾ teaspoons	8.5 milliliters
2 teaspoons	10 milliliters
1 tablespoon (½ fluid ounce)	15 milliliters
2 tablespoons (1 fluid ounce)	30 milliliters
¼ cup	60 milliliters
⅓ cup	80 milliliters
½ cup (4 fluid ounces)	120 milliliters
⅔ cup	160 milliliters
¾ cup	180 milliliters
1 cup (8 fluid ounces)	240 milliliters
1¼ cups	300 milliliters
1½ cups (12 fluid ounces)	360 milliliters
1⅔ cups	400 milliliters
2 cups (1 pint)	460 milliliters
3 cups	700 milliliters
4 cups (1 quart)	0.95 liter
1 quart plus ¼ cup	1 liter
4 quarts (1 gallon)	3.8 liters

LENGTH

1/8 inch	3 millimeters
¼ inch	6 millimeters
½ inch	1.25 centimeters
1 inch	2.5 centimeters
2 inches	5 centimeters
2 ½ inches	6 centimeters
4 inches	10 centimeters
5 inches	13 centimeters
6 inches	15.25 centimeters
12 inches (1 foot)	30 centimeters

WEIGHT

¼ ounce	7 grams
½ ounce	14 grams
¾ ounce	21 grams
1 ounce	28 grams
1 ¼ ounces	35 grams
1 ½ ounces	42.5 grams
1⅔ ounces	45 grams
2 ounces	57 grams
3 ounces	85 grams
4 ounces (¼ pound)	113 grams
5 ounces	142 grams
6 ounces	170 grams
7 ounces	198 grams
8 ounces (½ pound)	227 grams
16 ounces (1 pound)	454 grams
35¼ ounces (2⅕ pounds)	1 kilogram

OVEN TEMPERATURES

To convert Fahrenheit to Celsius, subtract 32 from Fahrenheit, multiply the result by 5, and then divide by 9.

Description	Fahrenheit	Celsius	British Gas Mark
Very cool	200°	95°	0
Very cool	225°	110°	¼
Very cool	250°	120°	½
Cool	275°	135°	1
Cool	300°	150°	2
Warm	325°	165°	3
Moderate	350°	175°	4
Moderately hot	375°	190°	5
Fairly hot	400°	200°	6
Hot	425°	220°	7
Very hot	450°	230°	8
Very hot	475°	245°	9

COMMON INGREDIENTS AND THEIR APPROXIMATE EQUIVALENTS

1 cup uncooked rice = 225 grams
1 cup all-purpose flour = 140 grams
1 stick butter (4 ounces • ½ cup • 8 tablespoons) = 110 grams
1 cup butter (8 ounces • 2 sticks • 16 tablespoons) = 220 grams
1 cup firmly packed brown sugar = 225 grams
1 cup granulated sugar = 200 grams

Information compiled from a variety of sources, including *Recipes into Type* by Joan Whitman and Dolores Simon (Newton, MA: Biscuit Books, 2000); *The New Food Lover's Companion* by Sharon Tyler Herbst (Hauppauge, NY: Barron's, 1995); and *Rosemary Brown's Big Kitchen Instruction Book* (Kansas City, MO: Andrews McMeel, 1998).

Index